HUMILITY'S DECEIT

CALVINO READING ARIOSTO READING CALVINO

WILEY FEINSTEIN

BORDIGHERA INCORPORATED
WEST LAFAYETTE, IN

PQ
4809
.A45
Z7
1995

© 1995 by Wiley Feinstein.

All rights reserved. Sections may be reprinted only by written permission from the author, and may not be reproduced for publication in book, magazine, or electronic media of any kind, except in quotations for purposes of literary reviews by critics.

Printed in the United States.

Published by
Bordighera, Inc.
Purdue University
1359 Stanley Coulter Hall
West Lafayette, IN 47907-1359

VIA FOLIOS 3
ISBN 1-884419-02-X

ACKNOWLEDGEMENTS

Computer diskettes that have not yet become defective never lie. My obsolete 5 1/4" floppies with the original files that have become this present book show that the text you are about to read, skim or sniff at was completed in July of 1988. I gratefully acknowledge the Leave of Absence I was granted by Loyola University Chicago's College of Arts and Science in Spring Semester 1988.

This winter, however, I was turned down when I requested another Leave of Absence. I felt hurt rejected betrayed humiliated devastated. But of course I shouldn't have. What other people think of you is of no importance of all. And I could probably have become the type of academic that all gets all the freebies he asks for. I just didn't, that's all. That's just the way it is. But what I really need to acknowledge is that thinking reading writing brooding in rejected isolation is the purest form known to man.

Wiley Feinstein
February 11, 1995

TABLE OF CONTENTS

INTRODUCTION(S)

Four Introductions for Four Different Kinds of Readers 1

    Introduction Number One. To the General Reader   1
    Introduction Number Two. To the Undergraduate Student   6
    Introduction Number Three A. For the Calvino Scholar   9
    Introduction Number Three B. For the Ariosto Scholar   10

CHAPTER ONE

If in a Summer Daze an Ariosto Professor 11

CHAPTER TWO

Checking Out Some College Girls 28

    Part One. Women in the Narrative Structure   32
    Part Two. Kissing Feminism Good-Bye   57

CHAPTER THREE

Laughing at the Writer-Boy's Madness 70

CHAPTER FOUR

Lies in Telling the Truth 87

CHAPTER FIVE

Can Calvino's Humility Really Not Be Proud? 114

    Part One. Ariosto Himself and Mr. Smogcloud   117
    Part Two. Bradamante and Ludmilla   119
    Part Three. Pin and Rodomonte   122
    Part Four. Orlando and Palomar   125

INDEX OF NAMES AND SUBJECTS 139

FOUR INTRODUCTIONS
FOR
FOUR DIFFERENT KINDS OF READERS
OF
HUMILITY'S DECEIT

(Note One: Please read *only* the introduction that applies to you personally and the interests that brought you to this book. We're on the honor system, and I urge you not to cheat.)

(Note Two: Come on! Of course you can read or skip whatever parts of this book you feel like. Reading is a free country. If you're in a hurry, skip to Chapter 4, pp. 87–113, the only pages I'm even remotely satisfied with.)

INTRODUCTION NUMBER ONE

To the General Reader

Somehow you've found this book lying around somewhere. Probably by chance in a public library. I don't know just where or just how and I have no idea what you're like as a person. But it's important to me to imagine that someone like you is reading this sentence right now.

Well, the first thing you have to do is promise me something. You have to promise that you won't close the book until you've read at least the next three paragraphs. Is that too much to ask?

All right, first of all, I have to tell you right away that this short book is all about the influence of a 16th-century Italian writer named Ludovico Ariosto on Italo Calvino, a 20th-century Italian writer that a lot of Americans who read important books have being reading lately.

Second of all, I want you to know that I wrote this book in order to amuse someone like you in particular. You're not a snob like some readers but a modest and thoughtful person who tries to laugh about some of the things we all take too seriously: (you know:) our problems in relating to the opposite sex, our problems with stupid romantic passions or other kinds of unrealistic dreams, our problems in understanding the world, ourselves and our limitations. Stuff like that.

Now I know you're thinking that those are things you're busy working out for yourself in your own way in your own life and that it's not really something you want a book to help you work out.

Well, fine. That's exactly what I hoped you'd think. And the fact is I didn't write this book in order to help you solve any of your real-life problems. Or even to help you understand yourself and your strange problems in new ways or something like that. No not at all.

Yes, I'm quite aware that people come in different ages, temperaments, degrees and kinds of adventurousness, combativeness, intellectuality etc. and have to develop their own real-life perspective on their own problems.

But there's another reason for raising serious questions and answering them in a certain way: in order to entertain and amuse a reader like you even as I show you that I respect your personal readerly freedom.

But let's go right to a sample specific serious question (S^3Q) so I can explain what I'm talking about.

SAMPLE SERIOUS QUESTION

> Can men ever learn new ways of thinking about women and relating to them in new and different ways?

SAMPLE UNSERIOUS ANSWER

> 1. Assume that the answer is a simple "YES! WHY NOT?," then, explain why and illustrate how this is so.
> 2. After you've given your yes answer (or even right in the middle of giving your yes answer) show that a "NO! OF COURSE NOT" answer is equally plausible.
> 3. Make sure that throughout your answer, you show that you're aware of the subjective prejudices that necessarily incinerate your objectivity. One way to do this is to allow yourself to get sidetracked in the middle of your discussion by matters of obsessive interest to you.

4. Go for all the laughs you can: because laughs provide the natural release for the frustrations that develop during your impossible quest for a more satisfying, less subjective answer.

You see, it's the carefully organized (but not too carefully organized) quest for an answer and the laughs that count in books like this one. And note how closely the two are related: laughter is the only possible tension-reliever once you (rightly or wrongly) convince yourself that there are no solutions to the serious problems you and I are really suffering over in our own partly miserable lives at this very moment.

Let's leave the sample question and get back to the general introduction itself.

As it turns out, the sample question I've used is in fact the basic question I ask and avoid answering in Chapter Two. Chapters Three, Four, and Five are not laid out as simply as Chapter Two but they too are based, basically, on playing the following serious questions for bookish tension-and-laughter effects:

Chapter Three: Can thinking about the madness of our desires help us to learn to control our longings to some extent?

Chapter Four: Is it true that all the "truths" about the world contained in the most highly-regarded books in our culture are false in important ways?

Chapter Five: Can we learn a significant kind of humility that we can remember to practice in our real life dealings with other people?

As this point I know you're thinking: what about Chapter One, and what about Ariosto and Calvino? Didn't you say that this book is about the influence of Ariosto on Calvino? Or was it Calvino's influence on Ariosto?

Yes, I did. Let me explain quite simply how these guys fit in. Thing is I've written the book for a reader like you who has no prior interest in Ariosto or Calvino. Even though it does happen to be quite true, as you might have already guessed, that Italo and Lodovico are interested in the same questions I am.

And it is also true that from my two authors, I steal my basic ideas about how to introduce and conclude a chapter, how to digress or slip in an unexpected reference to oneself and the present (in our case, the late 1980s here and now in the USA), how to write and joke about women, men, desire, truth, our egos, our jobs—but in

4—HUMILITY'S DECEIT

this book I try to make their ideas my own by applying them to my own life. So what I say about them is not important in and of itself: it's only important as a set up for my writing about my own problems and expressing my own versions of their ideas.

But why start out with previous writers in the first place, you ask? Or if you need previous writers, why not choose writers from our own country rather than from Italy?

Well, granted, you don't really need even to *start* with previous writers, much less write a whole book about two of them in particular. And granted, there are certain advantages to staying on your own side of the ocean when you pick authors to quote from.

But the thing is this: if you write about problems that people in the fairly distant past and in other countries have thought about, you can measure your ideas against theirs in interesting ways.

And secondly, it's comforting to have a problem like "Ariosto's Influence on Calvino" to have to try to work out, because even if it's not really that important to you or me in and of itself, it gives me a way of unifying this book by telling a gradually unfolding tale of two intriguing authors that is only complete on the last page.

(It's important to do various things to alleviate the monotony of whatever kind of book you're writing, not making it a boring one-track book. And of course I want you to keep in mind the general question of how my [and your] ideas are shaped [too much] by our favorite authors, filmakers, comedians etc.)

Another very important thing about the Ariosto and Calvino backbone of this book is that it makes me quote them regularly. And it's particular fun to play at translating a foreign author in a way that makes her yours personally and partly justifies stealing her stuff so shamelessly. I try to amuse you with some 1980s American conversational English translations of Calvino and Ariosto, that give you my idea of how funny and conversational they both are.

(For variety's sake, I'll sometimes give you more standard kinds of original translations to remind you of their different-ness and foreign-ness in time and space).

So that's about it. I think we can get started. Except I forgot: I still haven't said anything about Chapter One.

Well, Chapter One introduces you to both authors in its own way and more importantly, introduces you to my own way of (deceitfully and self-deceivingly) talking about myself and my profession.

I told you how important it is to try to consider one's own prejudices as much as possible. That's why I introduce myself right away as a literature-and-foreign-language professor with a certain self image in order to prepare you for how I'm going to be talking about myself and my problems all throughout the book. I happen to make a lot of complaints about what's wrong with my profession and how silly it is for everyone in it to take it so seriously. (Complaints you might very well make about your present job or a job you'll get in the future.)

But my purpose in complaining about my profession is not that I really want to urge people in it to try harder to make it a friendlier, more humane profession than it currently is. My purpose is really to study myself complaining and to celebrate comic complaining for its own sake. And show you of course—that I realize I'm not at all as outside the problem as I'd like to be and that there are a lot of reasons to complain about people like me.

Just as there are a lot of reasons to complain about people like you, too.

So if you like complaining and whining about being mistreated as much as I do and most people I know do . . .

(Yes, I am a fan of "It's Gary Shandling's show.")

you won't find this book a total waste of time, I hope.

INTRODUCTION NUMBER TWO

To the Undergraduate Student Who Has to Write a Literature Paper on Italo Calvino

Here you are in the library. You've brought half a dozen books on Calvino back to the public study carrel, including this one that the computer card-catalogue said was a study of the influence of Ariosto on Calvino.

It's 10:30 at night already. The five-page paper is due at 11:30 tomorrow and your instructor accepts "no late papers whatsoever." You've waited too long to start thinking about it. You'd do anything to make tonight last night. Going out to that stupid bar was an awful idea, wasn't it?

But don't worry. I'm not going to give you a lecture. I understand your problem and I sympathize with you. I think people should have as good a time in college as they can. Once you get a job, start a family . . . it's all over, it really is. You sense that because you have good instincts, good intuitive understanding, a lot of common sense. You know you're smarter than the 4.0 honor students who have already completely sacrificed their lives to their fear of failure in our mirthless society. And it so happens that your average isn't all that bad anyway, all things considered.

Well, you've opened the right book. You're in luck. Unless your boyfriend doesn't know how to word-process for you and you have no one to type it for you. . . . If that's the case you should have opened this at 6:15 p.m. Although, who knows, you might make it anyway. Go for it!

And don't worry about the instructions I'm going to give you making it too easy for your teacher to identify your paper as a last minute straight-out-of-Cliff-notes-or-the-equivalent job. I know your instructor's the type who makes it clear that no one can play HIM for a fool who can't recognize a fake when he sees one. So I'm giving instructions that he won't be able to pin down to this source. I mean if you're sharp enough to throw in the right variations, of course.

Calvino happens to be an easy author to write a quickie paper on. All you need to do is pick out a short story or a short chapter out of any novel he wrote after 1960 and then follow my instructions.

(The original copy-right date is on the page after the title page.) Maybe, I'd skip *Invisible Cities* or *Mr. Palomar*, if I were you. They're a little weird.

Here are the thinking and writing instructions:

I. THINKING INSTRUCTIONS:

1. Find quickly a story you seem to like and you can follow clearly.
2. Think about the main character(s) from the story: it might be the person who is talking about himself in the story, if there's an "I" in it.
3. Think about what happens to him or her.
4. Think about the lesson we learn about life or human nature: about things like how people relate to each other, make decisions, think about their problems etc.
5. Think specifically about anything humorous in the way the story is handled and about the way it ends or about what we learn at the end: and think about what importance humor or the ending might have.

II. WRITING INSTRUCTIONS:

First paragraph: identify the character and story you're going to write about and say when it was written. (Instructors are overly fond of dates—of all kinds!) Say something general about what happens to her/him and what we learn about life, human nature etc. from what happens.

Second paragraph: Tell all about the character(s) and her/ their qualities and/or way of thinking and make some observations about them. If you think anybody thinks too much or is too intellectual, say so. Don't be afraid!

Paragraphs 3–5: Tell what happens to him/her/them and what we learn about life or human nature from the story. Don't call it a lesson, though. Be subtle!

Next paragraph: Write about how the humor or the ending or something strange or surprising about the story affects the lesson and our overall perspective on what happens (to do this you might need to ask a more studious classmate for general info about the book that the particular Calvino story you've chosen is in.)

Draw some wise conclusions about everything you've said so far. But restrain yourself: don't be too wise or say general things that have nothing to do with the story. Finally, take as much time as you can to think up a cute title. (Don't underestimate the importance of titles. And don't take the title of this book as a particularly good example. You can do better!)

(If the paper isn't long enough, maybe you'll have to compare or contrast a couple of different characters from different stories: add the info about character #2 paragraph by paragraph: it's so easy in the age of word-processors.)

Well that's all I can think of. I haven't really tested out the instructions very carefully, so they might not work at all. But even if they don't work, they might get you started. I hope you get an "A," I really do. You deserve one.

INTRODUCTION NUMBER THREE A
For the Calvino Scholar

This is a study of the influence of Ariosto on Calvino that can't possibly interest a person like you.

But I know you're not sure you can take my word for it. Even though the bibliography on Calvino has been exploding lately, you still think you can manage to read everything—even though it's all so disappointing and so easy to dismiss on account of its lack of sophistication or excess of sophistication.

But I really don't want you to spend your valuable reading time on this. You see, I'm just a real reader-friendly kind of guy and I think I know the type of thing that interests you and the type of thing that doesn't.

So here's why you don't need to read this book:

1. The book has no bibliography or footnotes and its approach is not directly derived from careful reading of Foucault, Lacan, Derrida, Guattari or similar (Non) Authorities.
2. The book explain nowhere either of the following:
    a. How it relates to other recent books on Calvino and similar authors.
    b. How it relates to other more general recent books that treat the same kinds of subjects.
3. The book contains some irresponsible translations of Calvino into too-contemporary an American idiom.

If you turn the page and read further, don't say I didn't warn you.

INTRODUCTION NUMBER THREE B

For the Ariosto Scholar

This is a study of the possible influence of Calvino on the way we read Ariosto that can't possibly interest a person like you.

But I know you're not sure you can take my word for it. Even though the bibliography on Ariosto has been increasing steadily of late and is getting a little harder to keep under control, you still know you can handle it all—even though it's all so disappointing and so easy to dismiss on account of either its lack or excess of sophistication.

But I really don't want you to spend your valuable reading time on this. You see, I'm just a real reader-friendly kind of guy and I think I know what interests you and what doesn't.

But I know you want specific reasons, so let me give you some:

1. The book has no bibliography or footnotes and its approach is not derived from careful reading of either recent general (Non)Authorities or recent Ariosto criticism.
2. The book explains nowhere either of the following:
a. How it relates to other recent books on Ariosto and similar authors.
b. How exactly it relates to certain other recent books on literature that treat the same kinds of problems.
3. The book contains some irresponsible translations of Ariosto into too-contemporary an American idiom.

If you turn the page and read further, don't say I didn't warn you.

CHAPTER ONE

IF IN A SUMMER DAZE AN ARIOSTO PROFESSOR

It has been common in our century for writers and professors like me to shun like the plague the adjective "professorial." For those of us intellectuals with a REAL Interest in the Mind's TRUE Liberation, something professorial is something joyless, conventional, and brain-deadening.

Heaven forbid that we should speak of academic mirthlessness when we discuss the labors of love of certain Joyous Artists or Passionate Intellectuals! Perish the thought that we suggest that certain revolutionary writers and professors are not substantially different from the so many Professor Gravity Grimsly types you see walking toward class with an absurd air of self-importance in the decaying Humanities Building on your average American campus.

James Joyce—someone whose mediocre opinions outside of his fiction are quoted far too frequently—jokes that his last two (excruciatingly long) novels "will keep the professors busy for years." In his self-delusion, he is unable to realize that all his novels show a typical boring literature professor's interests and temperament in countless ways and that his continuing popularity with English professors and graduate students is certainly based more on his professoriality than on anything important he has to say.

Joyce's remarks alone ought to convince us that nowadays we must drop the distinction between the All Too Few "anti-professorial" writers, teachers, and intellectuals and the Rest of the Rabble: between, on the one hand, the Few Beautiful Souls and, on the other hand, the Soulless Many who publish and perish senselessly throughout long pointless careers.

I'm sorry I don't have time to confront the issue of why I just felt the need to take a cheap shot at James Joyce. But I mean . . . Calvino himself gave me the idea when he once liquidated James by calling him "too much the adolescently blaspheming Catholic who, furthermore . . ."

But wait a minute! What am I doing? Why should I need Calvino's authority to justify what I say? I mean if *he's* always telling us not to trust anyone else's truths, don't I have to take full responsibility for whatever stupid opinions of his I parrot or decide not to parrot?

But actually, now that I remember, one of this chapter's main points is going to be that, Calvino, like all writers and professors (although admittedly to a much lesser extent than me) can be outright stupid and boring on many occasions. For in this chapter, I'm going to be quoting some of Calvino's remarks about the *Orlando Furioso* and then point out how barrenly professorial and listlessly conventional Calvino gets anytime he writes about Ariosto.

(Special Parenthetical Justification That There Are Various Reasons To Skip: It so happens it is quite fair to level the charge of "overly professorial" at Italo Calvino. He himself once insulted Pier Paolo Pasolini by calling him "by far the most professorial of all us Italian writers." Calvino must have meant that one can easily be cynical about Pasolini's attempts to identify with the blasphemingly energized bad-boy characters in novels like *A Violent Life* who say things like "fuck *that* motherfuckin' shit" in Roman dialect at least twice per page, if not more. As if it weren't clear that Pasolini has a Linguistics Professor's interest in ghetto slang! Not to mention a banal Marxist Professor's ideas about the praiseworthy vitality of the illiterate or less-educated folk. And, to tell a little more of the story, Calvino's insult is merely a retort to Pasolini's liquidatingly dismissive remark that Calvino is a boring "enlightened Piedmontese" rationalist.)

(But—if you want to know what I think—I'm of the opinion that insults in print are no big deal or anything and that if you feel like insulting me after reading this book or even before finishing another sentence, it won't bother me at all. As long as you never come up to me and actually punch me out. But I think we professors can stop pretending that we and our favorite writers are all "basically nice guys" who are somehow less fucked-up and less full of BIG PSYCHOLOGICAL PROBLEMS than everyone else.)

Wait a minute! Didn't I just now (I mean before the parenthetical remark) slip into using the terms "professorial" and "conventional" almost as if I believed they were things that could and should be overcome?? Well, fact is—and I'm sure you'll agree—if you think it over enough—that any kind of writing or teaching is inescapably full of conventional professoriality and professorial conventionality.

But I am going to accept the negative rhetorical use of the terms for a specific reason in this chapter and for a general reason in the book as a whole. Here they are:

THE SPECIFIC REASON:
The distinction professors/anti-professors is rhetorically useful for me in this particular chapter. At the climactic point that begins on page 25, I'm going to pose some somewhat dramatic rhetorical questions to Calvino in phonily impassioned response to his astonishingly boring remarks about Ariosto and the *Orlando Furioso*. In order for these rhetorical questions to be effective, you have to accept conventionally conventional ideas about conventionality and the truths that lie outside of stifling scholarly conventions.

THE GENERAL REASON:
But here's the really important reason: however emphatically I intellectually reject the division of writers and professors into True and False ones, I still have an emotional need for this phony distinction in order to think of myself as a writer and teacher. I mean . . . think of my own personal history: I was an undergraduate student in the early 1970s and demonstrated vaguely against the Vietnam war and liked the song "Imagine" by John Lennon ("Imagine no professors, it's easy if you try, no jerks looming over lecterns, above us only sky.") and still today I wear my hair long and flowing on my shoulders, or sometimes in a pony tail. Get serious! How can I not be basically in the right? And so the fact remains that in this book I'm going to be trying to be as thoroughly anti-professorial as much as I can. Even though reason should dissolve all such fantasies.

O.K. . . . Relax! We're very near beginning the real part of the chapter.

Except . . . there's one more thing I have to get off my chest. Let me remind you that my nasty attacks on Calvino and his professoriality and bad ideas in this chapter will be integrated, contradicted, balanced and buried by the hundred of paragraphs with conflicting ideas in the four following chapters in which I'll often be showing my appreciation and admiration of an author who on some days I sometimes think has been really important in helping me learn to laugh a little at life's dreariness.

I mean I feel a little uneasy starting out what I might possibly want to be a kind of sunny-in-spite-of-everything book like this by cloudily suggesting that Calvino has real problems busting Ariosto's largely-looming ironic ghost or anything. Or that I myself, mellow person that I always am in real life, (can't you tell by the way I write?) have any problems dealing with Calvino or have any need to cut him down to my small size in some way by showing that I have more interesting things to say about Ariosto than he did. Or that Ariosto is much smarter than everybody and that *only I* understand just how and that Calvino—and everybody else for that matter—doesn't understand shit about shit. I mean just about Ariosto, that is.

All right then. Now we can start. My pre-amblin' ramblin' and pre-ludin' broodin' are all over. The sad moment when promise turns into disappointment has come. Since we all know or should know that fulfillment does not exist and that if it did we wouldn't know what it was.

All right we're ready for the real start of this chapter. Which is about what, you ask?

Well, what I want to do is start talking about the world of the *Orlando Furioso* and its influence on Calvino by quoting for you some of Calvino's major comments on Ariosto's long poem. As I quote them, I'll be telling you right away what's wrong with Calvino's way of looking at Ariosto.

Specifically, I'm going to be accusing Italo Calvino rather scoffingly of chewing on and digesting much too much received opinion and not allowing himself to properly develop an instinctive idea he had about the energy that moves Ariosto's principal characters:

> E' un'energia volta verso l'avvenire, ne sono sicuro, non verso il passato quella che muove Orlando, Angelica, Ruggiero, Bradamante, Astolfo . . .

> (It's an energy turned toward the future, I'm sure of it, not towards the past that moves Orlando, Angelica, Ruggiero, Bradamante, Astolfo . . .)

Oh yes, I should tell you that he had also early on (1958 when he was 35) acknowledged just how important Ariosto was to him:

> "Tra tutti i poeti della nostra tradizione quello che sento più vicino e nello stesso tempo più oscuramente affascinante è Ludovico Ariosto e non mi stanco mai di rileggerlo"
>
> ("Among all the poets of our tradition, the one I feel closest to and at the same time obscurely fascinating is Ludovico Ariosto and I never tire of re-reading him")

But anytime he later on writes about the *Furioso*, Calvino avoids probing that obscure fascination or the personal meaning Ariosto's "futurity" might have for him.

But right now, before we go any further and start looking at the specifics of Calvino's uninspired comments about Ariosto, you need to know something about the received opinion that Calvino accepts too readily.

Well here's the story. For say, the last hundred and twenty-five years or so, (mostly) male Italian Literature professors have been showing off their impressive historical intelligence and chivalrically romancing the women in their classes by explaining that Ariosto's *Orlando Furioso*, an Ironic Epic of Chivalry, is a natural product of The Highest Height of the High Italian High Renaissance (hereafter abbreviated as H3IHR).

Ariosto, they tell their feverishly note-taking students, takes up legendary medieval subject matter that had, first of all, been found in two distinct genres in the rich Medieval French literary tradition that began to get going soon after the year 1000.

(Why the year 1000 and not before? Who knows? I would suppose for the usual economic and political reasons: you know, there was a need for literature to justify certain political classes, to entertain lounging men and women of letters who lived in at least reasonably good neighborhoods and needed to bury their eyes in books so as to avoid having to look at the large numbers of underprivileged people their society forced suffering upon.)

But let's not get off the subject or get nostalgic over societal-criticism talk that we now all agree is always the same and always pointless for depressing reasons I don't want to get into.

But wait a minute. Before I get into specific details about where Ariosto steals his medieval chivalric material from, let me make some general remarks to help you think about *why* he and his readers might be attracted to chivalric heroes and heroines and their adventures. You know what I'm talking about: adventures in which knights of old fight for their king's honor or to rescue damsels in distress from bad men or monsters, or try to win jousts to prove themselves worthy of their ladies' true love and stuff like that.

In general I can tell you that readers in Ariosto's day were as comfortably at home with chivalric characters and their stories as we readers or viewers nowadays are with detective stories or soap operas and baseball games and their stories. Or it might be even better to talk about magic-filled tv cartoons and their audiences.

(Yes, I do happen to have an almost-seven-year-old that watches quite a few of them.)

Because children who watch cartoons quickly learn to feel at home with a very fixed, predictable and—in a word—traditional system of rules and values.

Take a cartoon like "Jem and the Holograms," a cartoon series about an all-woman pop-music group. When we watch "Jem and the Holograms," we escape into a world of "fun, fashion and fame" where Jem and her cartoon rock co-stars are the good gals (pretty, honest, hard-working, sincere, kind) and where Pzazz and the Misfits (ugly, dishonest, lazy, false, nasty) are the bad gals. We know what cluster of values the young women in each of the rival groups represent and we are always pleased when Jem uses her magic powers of Synergy to make things turn out well for her and her friends and bad for Pzazz and the Misfits.

Well the chivalric world that Ariosto makes use of is a kind of magic-filled cartoon world of good-guy Christian Knights and bad-guy Pagan Infidels . . . and good and bad women too, of course. We readers are the children who know who's who and what values the characters stand for and who's going to win in the end: we know that men and women with correct chivalric values (who are, that is, honest, kind, courageous, and faithful to family, friend, lover and country)—will be rewarded and the bad guys—especially the most evil ones (totally lacking in chivalric virtue: dishonest, nasty, unkind, cowardly, faithless) will get the punishment and the defeats they deserve.

But it is of course true that Ariosto (and Calvino often) use a children's-story kind of world with seemingly simple traditional characters and standard kinds of adventures to write books for adults even sophisticated ones who have studied with Overrated Professors.

Now, aside from the fact that Ariosto and Calvino are reminding us that we're all regressing into childhood anytime we open up a literary work or work of literary criticism—there is another important reason for them to choose a cartoon-like world. You see, both authors are overly fond (as we'll see) of a certain kind of total ironic skepticism about values.

Let me take a separate paragraph to explain about this kind of skepticism.

A Value-Free Totalitarian Skeptic Author (Hereafter VF-TSA) is not sure exactly what she wants to affirm or deny in her writing. But one of the forces that drives her to write is her desire to raise unanswerable general questions about moral value systems and how we think about ourselves in relation to them, questions such as:

> (1): Are we sure that trying to live according to the demands of traditional moral value systems (or immoral-value countersystems) is the right idea? And if so, why?
>
> (2): Why is it that we need to think in terms of traditional value systems or anti-traditional value systems in the first place? Could we ever learn to stop thinking of ourselves as some sort of right-valued hero or heroine in some sort of terribly silly story?

You can see that if you're gonna be a VF-TSA, you want to start with a world just like those in which young people in our culture are still taught values. In this manner, of course, it's easy to raise all the doubts and questions you possibly can.

All right. Enough useless generalizing about why fairy tale worlds or legendary worlds might attract authors like Ariosto and Calvino. Now we can go back to looking more specifically at where Ariosto's world comes from.

I was talking about two medieval French literary genres that Ariosto is dependent on when he writes his very long (1000-page) Renaissance poem. Specifically these two literary kinds are:

GENRE NUMBER ONE
Legendary Sports Heroes

In this genre, you find heroes like Roland in the French hit *Song of Roland*, a song that was enormously popular in 12th-century Paris discos. As he fights the infidels who threaten Christendom, Roland is courageous, self-sacrificing, accepting of duty, physically and mentally tough, faithful to friend and cause, a real team player. He gives to king Charlemagne the kind of effort that present-day athletes put out for the coach. In short, Roland has all the positive qualities that t.v. sportscasters and coaches on commercials urge us to develop as much as we can (I guess) so that we'll be best prepared to do our absolute best in the Great Struggles for Sweet Victory we must face in our own careers.

GENRE NUMBER TWO
"All My Children": Medieval Style

In this genre, in stories like "Lancelot and Guenivere," we have knights in heat and damsels on ice who need melting: desperate passion and lust and of course no end of murderous jealousy and frantic idiotic self-torturing. Thrown in with the love stuff, for variety's sake, are the other kinds of things we still now associate naturally with medieval knights and the ladies they loved (usually in vain): dragons and monsters and other mythical beasts, remarkably trusty horses, enchanted swords helmets lances shields and armor, rings that make you invisible, flying horselike creatures and enchanted castles and islands. And good and bad male and female magicians and wizards anytime a dazzling special effect or exciting plot development is needed—so that readers feel they are getting their money's worth.

By the time in the 1500s that Ariosto decides to write about knights and ladies it seems like they've been around forever. Just like mystery novels and sit-coms or stupid tv talk shows and beer commercials and car ads seem to us like they've always been here. So it's a good time for an intellectual author to joke around with these characters and their typical stories. Just like nowadays intellectual writers play around with mysteries or soaps nowadays and the predictable things that always happen in them.

Oh, I forgot, you might be rather vague on the Renaissance in general and the "High Renaissance" in particular and might want to know more about what it was like to live in the early 1500s when Ariosto wrote. Well—to be honest—it's hard to know very much about what it was really like. But since Calvino's going to be talking in old-fashioned historical terms, I'd better give you some idea of things we professors usually say when we talk about the 1500s.

If the idea of "High Renaissance" is new to you, go find an art book with reproductions of paintings by Raphael, like "The School of Athens" "The Dispute over the Holy Sacrament," or one of his many paintings of just-like-the-REAL-virgin Madonnas Even though Raphael Sanzio is born nine years later than Ludovico Ariosto, it so happens that he paints all his most famous masterpieces in just the same 10 year period (1505–1515) during which 30–40 year old Ariosto is toiling away late at night at the First Edition of *Orlando Furioso*.

(All right I know you didn't really look at a Raphael painting. It would have taken too much effort. But it doesn't really matter. We can go on anyways.)

Now look at a description from Ariosto, one of a character sweetly-named Medoro:

> Medoro avea la guancia colorita
> e bianca e grata ne la età novella
> e fra la gente a quella impresa uscita
> non era faccia più gioconda e bella.
> Occhi avea neri, e chioma crespa d'oro
> angel parea di quei del sommo coro.
>
> (Medoro's cheeks were wonderfully colored
> and pleasingly white in the glory of his youth.
> Why, in that entire army out on its mission
> you'd find no face more sweet, no face more fine!
> He had black eyes and hair with curls or gold:
> An angel—you'd swear it!—right out of the seraphs fold!)

O.K. then, if you're talkin' Renaissance, you're talkin' strikingly beautiful people, strikingly beautiful art, no question about it. In Raphael and Ariosto you note immediately that both artists love beautiful forms a very great deal (in Raphael, groups of beautiful ideal people act out a story; in Ariosto beautiful sequences of stanzas describe beautiful ideal people and tell stories). You can get the idea that form is much more important than content to Raphael and Ariosto.

This of course can go along very well with ironic skepticism: I mean, reread carefully that description of Medoro. (Or don't if you don't have time.) Don't you suspect immediately that Medoro is *too* beautiful and that Ariosto might not end up taking him and the perfect moral qualities he's going to have wholly seriously? And don't you suspect that Raphael might be uninterested in or even skeptical about teaching religious lessons about, say, the religious essence of the Madonna's humility?

But let's move on. Now you'll want to know how the High Renaissance relates to the rest of the period, won't you?

Well, a term like High Renaissance implies that a period like the Renaissance must at some point rise (however much it tries to hold back) to an orgasmic climax before sadly falling into limp oblivion. After which a new period will get the urge to be born, grow old too quickly and die.

You probably know that the name Renaissance or "Born Again Not Always Christian Period" (which I'm applying to the years 1400–1615) refers to the supposed "rebirth" of classical yuppie-chic taste in art and poetry after a long period as full of uncouth, immature medievality as the action on the field and in the stands during a typical Bears' football game at Soldier Field in Chicago.

But the Renaissance can be looked at as a period with stages that rises to its absolute height just in time for Ariosto to write the *Orlando Furioso* and begins to fall immediately after his death.

(Pay attention here: you need to know this in order to make sense out of what Calvino is going to say about Ariosto.)

Here, we're talking specifically about Ariosto's Renaissance interest in medieval stories and values that he's not sure whether we can ever outgrow or not (period stories are always about growing up with respect—or rather lack of respect—to the more or less recent past). To know just where to place Ariosto, we would need to compare and contrast his particular High Renaissance way of looking at Medieval Values and Styles with the way, let's say, one earlier Not-Quite-So-High Renaissance author and one later Downright Lowdown Renaissance man looked at them.

And it so happens we're in luck. It so happens we've got Matteo Maria Boiardo on the not-quite-so-high side and Miguel

Saavedra de Cervantes on the (too) late side of the Renaissance to show us exactly why Ariosto fits in where he does.

(There are many other Renaissance authors [or close-to-the-Renaissance authors] you can compare/contrast Ariosto to besides Boiardo and Cervantes: if you want to know who they are go to a university library and look up Ariosto [as subject] on the computerized catalogue—I mean if you have nothing better to do. But I'm choosing Boiardo and Cervantes just to prepare you for what Calvino says. And remember that the clear differences between Ariosto and Boiardo and Cervantes I'll be kind of "accepting" for the moment are ones I'll be placing into doubt as soon as I start quoting Calvino.)

Matteo Maria Boiardo vs. Ariosto:

Towards the ends of the first really unmistakably Reborn Century, the 15th to be exact, a poet in the then flourishing city of Ferrara named Matteo Maria Boiardo writes the *Orlando Innamorato*. Well, the fact is that everything I said about Ariosto taking and putting together material from two old French genres and being pretty ironic about the whole business, I could have said about Boiardo, the leading poet of the generation before Ariosto, born just 33 years before Ludovico Ariosto. And I haven't even told you that the *Orlando Furioso* is actually a direct continuation of the *Orlando Innamorato*.

At first glance, in our comparison of Boiardo and Ariosto, we see two very similar poets—I mean as long as we're talkin' basic subject matter, basic storytellin' and basic ironic attitudes. But when Boiardo writes, the time is not yet ripe for knowing how to write in a hyper-sophisticated style in which you non-chalantly show off your dazzling artistic control of a stunningly varied narration.

But aside from that kind of technical difference, Boiardo and Ariosto are pretty much the same. For in general, both the *Orlando Innamorato* and the *Orlando Furioso* are exuberantly Renaissancey enough in spirit to be worthy of the period whose artworks and architecture we still seek out amid the crowds on our silly trips to Italy in the age of mass tourism.

(And of course it's not as if professor types didn't ruin tourist-trap countries like modern Italy by their presence. Professors like me are no better than the regular idiot tourists and "partying abroad" ugly American students like the ones we send from Loyola University of Chicago send to our joke of a Rome Center where no one ever speaks a word of Italian outside of Italian class and no student who has ever gone there has ever read a word of Ariosto. Which is of course just the way I want it to be so that I can feel a certain stupid kind of superiority that helps keep me going—don't misunderstand me.)

So—I repeat—the only difference between Boiardo and Ariosto is that Ariosto has this awesome stylistic sophistication and stunning ability to weave many sub-plots together in the beautiful overall architecture that he fits all his interconnected stories into. But that little difference might be enough to make all the difference in the world for effective ironizing. Or maybe it doesn't make all that much difference at all. . . . But gosh!—that's enough Boiardo. Now I'd better move on to Cervantes, many people's favorite author in the world and one I myself immensely enjoyed reading a few years back.

Cervantes and Ariosto:

We compare Miguel de Cervantes with Ludovico Ariosto to learn something about the essence of Ariosto's non-tragic spirit in his attitude towards the medieval chivalric values and virtues, (which if I haven't said yet I mize well say now are as I understand them not all that different from the values and virtues we Americans have to measure our image of ourselves against).

Cervantes' *Don Quijote* is also a book no more and no less than Ariosto's about knights of old and battles for the sake of truth and justice and public glory and personal honor as well as stories about the astonishingly thin real-world foundations on which lovers build love stories in their imaginations. And like Ariosto, Cervantes writes with a style and technical sophistication that is dazzlingly High Renaissance.

But—just like Boiardo—Cervantes is only a half-twin of Ariosto. In this case, we just have to reverse the terms a little. With Cervantes, it's the overtly cynical attitude towards medieval chivalry and all its ideals that is different. Cervantes shows clearly that it is incredibly hard to live according to any sort of ideals in the brutal real world. Cervantes, poor guy, has a vastly and tragically profound spirit. Although's he inside the Renaissance as far as style goes, Cervantes is already quite outside of Ariosto's optimistic period as far as content goes.

It's as if this Spanish dude had already developed a modern case of the Chicago Blues. He writes as if he gets his sense of what real life is like from standing on a crowded mean El train in Chicago on an icy wind cold winter Monday morning: absorbing Total Desolation Vibes (hereafter TDV) from a hopeless train—carload of grimly hostile commuters.

Enough second-stage preamble. Sorry if it was too long. It was just the minimum necessary for you to understand Calvino's remarks about Ariosto that we now turn to.

Problem #1: What is the relation between Boiardo and Ariosto?

> "Ma soprattutto l'*Innamorato* fu oscurato dal *Furioso* cioé dalla continuazione che Ludovico Ariosto intraprese a scrivere una decina d'anni dopo la morte del Boiardo, una continuazione che fu subito tutt'altra cosa: dalla ruvida scorza quattrocentesca il Cinquecento esplode come una lussureggiante vegetazione carica di fiori . . ."

> (But above all the *Innamorato* was obscured by the *Furioso*, I mean by the continuation that L. Ariosto undertook to write about ten years after Boiardo's death, a continuation that was instantly something else entirely: from the rough 15th-century outer covering, the sixteenth century explodes like a luxurious growth of vegetation all full of flowers)

What is evident in this passage is the extreme sharpness of classification. The *Furioso* is "entirely a different matter" than the *Innamorato*. It's as neatly in its century as the *Furioso* is in its. The change in the first two digits 14— to 15— makes for magical transformations. But come on, Professor Calvino, is Ariosto that clearly and that safely different from Boiardo? Are there no fruits and flowers in Boiardo? Is he that unrefined? Aren't you in an awful hurry to put authors in their proper places? Aren't you slipping too easily into a game of differences and contrasts? Are you sure you had time to read the *Innamorato* carefully given all the projects you were busy on?

24—HUMILITY'S DECEIT

Problem #2: What is Ariosto's attitude towards the medieval material he takes up in the *Furioso*?:

> Gli storici della letteratura hanno molto discusso su quale era l'atteggiamento di Ariosto verso il passato medievale che è la materia del suo poema e in particolare verso la cavalleria. Pur vedendo le gesta dei suoi eroi attraverso l'ironia e la trasfigurazione favolosa, egli non tende mai a sminuire le virtú cavalleresche, non abbassa mai la statura umana che quegli ideali presuppongono, anche se a lui ormai pare non resti altro che farne pretesto per un gioco grandioso e appassionante ... Ariosto sembra un poeta limpido, ilare e senza problemi ...
>
> (Literary historians have greatly debated over what the attitude of Ariosto was towards the Medieval past that was the subject matter of his poem and in particular towards the institution of Chivalry. Even in viewing the great actions of his heroes ironically and through his transfigurations of fantasy, he never tends to belittle chivalric virtues, he never lowers the human stature that those ideals presuppose, even though it seems clear to him that by his time there is nothing more to do with them (chivalric ideals) than to use them as a pretext for a grandiose, impassioning game. Ariosto seems a clear-minded poet, good-humored and untroubled ...)

Are you sure it's the right idea necessarily to worry about what historians of literature or professors in general have "greatly debated"? Sometimes, as in your prefaces and essays, you can be as highly cynical as I'm trying to be in this book about standard discussions about literature ... Aren't you awfully quick to make Ludovico into a clear-spirited, good-humored, untroubled man of good-humored untroubled times? Is that really all there is to him? Are you sure he never undermines chivalric virtues or never suggests that he harbors very disturbing doubts about our noble "human stature"? And can't you explain a little more about this big game you say Ariosto is playing with his chivalric material and its heroes and heroines and values? Isn't your affirmative, assertive language in an awful hurry to suppress any kind of complex discussion about Ariosto and his supposed "good-natured" optimism. And can't you try a little harder to generalize outside of historical categorizes about why Ariosto writes about a system of values from the past he obviously doesn't wholly believe in? I very much like your use of the word "pretext." It is just the right word. But what if looking for pretexts for playing games is the fate of all writers and intellectuals? Aren't you in fact worried that the idea of literary (or literary critical) content as mere pretext for enigmatic (and not really justifiable) game playing is precisely the idea of literature you develop more and more clearly as your own career develops?

Problem #3: What is the difference between Ariosto and Cervantes?:

> Ariosto è certamente lontano dalla profondità tragica che avrà Cervantes, quando un secolo dopo, lui compirà la dissoluzione della letteratura cavalleresca
>
> (Ariosto is certainly far from the tragic profundity that Cervantes will have, when a century afterwards in the *Don Quijote* he will complete the dissolution of chivalric literature.)

Professor, you speak of the dissolution of chivalric literature in Cervantes? How can you have read the *Furioso* and not seen that it had *already* completed the dissolution of chivalric literature? (Or why not maybe even say that Boiardo had already completely dissolved it, for that matter?) And why only chivalric literature? Why not all literature that wants to teach us something significant about how to live or how best to understand or accept reality in its menacing complexity? Is there really a primitive period before the dissolution of literature or isn't it always (as soon as it starts) dissolving itself in self-doubts and self-irony? Or shouldn't we say playing a phony game of dissolving itself in self-doubts and self-irony? Which is going to be your game, just as it's the game of all confident people who play phony insecurity games, huh? And what about this business of tragic profundity? Isn't there something tragically profound about taking up medieval subject matter as a mere pretext for play, which is what you yourself say about what Ariosto does? Why are you forcing Ariosto into the role of untroubled poet and making him the opposite of

Cervantes? Can their works be put so neatly in categories? Aren't you suppressing questions, gliding over the complex nature of irony as sweeping as you show you understand Ariosto's to be, trying to create neat differences between authors of different periods that might not be nearly so sharp? I could even point out a certain strange remark Cervantes has his hero himself make about Ariosto in which he seems to understand that what he's doing in the *Quijote* is the same as what Ariosto did in the *Furioso* and in which he also shows he understands that it doesn't matter at all ... I wish I had the time.

But could it be true that you need such distinctions *in order to think of yourself* as a late 20th-century author with an appropriate kind of tragic profundity? Are you perhaps afraid you yourself aren't tragically profound enough for the late twentieth century? What if I said that you often seem to me basically as good-natured and optimistic in your game-playing as you say Ariosto is in his?

Whew! All those questions have worked me up into a sweat! Who knows why? What does it matter, anyway, figuring out whether it's more useful to consider authors as distinct and separate from one another, neatly arising in a very specific period or as dangerously similar or even virtually identical if you can learn to cut through surface differences. (Lately I've been picking up recent books by Primo Levi and Giorgio Manganelli and finding them partly indistinguishable from Calvino's: every other page or so I see something Calvino could have written).

Well this book is taking the latter route to the limit, I mean, the no-essential-differences-between-Ariosto-and-Calvino route. It's based on a wildly anti-conventional notion (ha! ha!) that in all the things that count in literature Ariosto and Calvino are just the same.

So that's about it for this chapter. I need to rest before I come out for the next round. Just one more thing, though: let me warn you modern lovers of debunking-books that I'm not really interested in belaboring Calvino's paranoid refusal to face his enormous affinities with Ariosto. No, I have no warped envious need to minimize Calvino's achievement. So I won't say a thing more about Calvino's running away from truths he could and should have faced about the nature of his debt to Ariosto. Or say that, for all the acclaim Calvino could receive from a Book-Review reading world much too quickly pleased with the latest fictional consumer novelty, he is in truth a Totally Unnecessary Inferior Imitation of Ariosto who had already done it all much better in much wiser times for literature and art. No, no, no: no such claim will be made. Don't worry. Just relax and keep reading.

And one last thing: I should probably say simply that it could well be that Calvino comes up with his hurried received-idea intro to Ariosto (mostly full of long quotes from the *Furioso*) simply because he had taken on too many commitments at a particularly active moment in his career in the late nineteen sixties, a period in which there were a lot more interesting things to do than read Ariosto and rethink his importance.

Nowadays, frankly, there really isn't anything better to do. There really isn't.

But now it's time to *really* begin this book. But first I want you to listen to a song. No, not the "Me and My Friends Are Jem Girls" theme. (Although that might be relevant to next chapter too, come to think of it.) It's a song that is on side one of an old Beach Boys album called "Summer Days" that is also on a pretty recent album by David Lee Roth. So please don't turn the page until after you've bopped your head to the neanderthal beat of the song "California Girls" and thought about the song a minute.

🙵

CHAPTER TWO

CHECKING OUT SOME COLLEGE GIRLS

The song "California Girls," one of the few truly great songs of the legendary 1960's, is a song that countless male American University students have adapted and applied to young women on their own campuses. In creating their own version of the hit recording, male students imagine that the different characteristics celebrated by the Beach Boys can be applied to women students of different dorms or sorority houses or even of different majors, clubs, or activities groups.

In "California Girls," the Beach Boys sing about what there is to dig (as one used to say) in four basic non-California types of American women: east-coast girls are "hip" and stylish in their dress, southern girls can knock you out "with the way they talk," midwest farmer's daughters can "really make you feel all right," and northern girls with their kisses of fire can "keep their boyfriends warm at night."

After the basic list, the Beach Boys continue on dreamily about how west coast girls "all get so tanned" and about how they dig Hawaiian Island girls because of their bikinis.

This song is addressed to a male listener's fantasy (like mine) and gives pretty much all the things we boys cherish women for. The effect of the song (constructed with brilliant poetic control: note how the northern girls and their torrid fantasy kiss are dreamt of at the climax of the first stanza) is to create a composite imaginary ideal woman.

The particular fantasy that delightfully dances in my mind whenever I hear "California Girls" is this: I dream that a young woman with the hipness of an easterner, the tan of a Californian, the accent of a southerner, the down-home charm of a midwesterner and the hot lips of a northern girl will one day walk right into one of my Italian language or lit classes.

(But I wonder if I'd be able to figure out what type of dream lover figure she was looking for in a male college professor . . . Or whether I could adapt myself to suit *her* fantasies, whatever they are precisely. But I doubt it. With my limitations, I really doubt it.)

But let's not dwell on depressing subjects. Let's get back to the Beach Boys: I now ask you to allow me to pretend for a moment that I'm the kind of Serious Intellectual Who Knows His Dates Well And Has A Professional Sense Of Just Where We've Been In Relation To The Disastrous Place We Are Unfortunately In Just Now.

Because if you allow me to pretend that, I'll say that we ought to attach great historical significance to the song California Girls on account of its particular original release date (1966 June 6th, 6 p.m.) and subsequent revival date (1984, Aug. 6th 11:58 p.m.). Because—in between the Beach Boys original (on the album "Summer Daze") and the repetition by David Lee Roth in 1984—radical feminism's challenge (in America and elsewhere) to male dominance rises and falls.

(Note again that once you define a period or a movement you also have to assign or predict its date of death).

After 1984, our "post-feminist" culture shrugs its shoulders and stops worrying about redefining women and changing their traditional aspirations. For example, I'm told that most young women students at Loyola University of Chicago (where I teach, in case you've forgotten) are here exclusively to find a husband.

(Which of course is not necessarily a reason to shake one's head in Deep Consternation. In my opinion, as you'll see throughout this book, anyone who finds any way whatsoever to avoid thinking in terms of "Personal Fulfillment in a Rewarding Career" must be on the right track.)

In this chapter (in case you're starting to wonder), I'm going to look at Ariosto and Calvino's identical way of playing with hypothetical feminist possibilities before I come right out and say something that's, frankly, highly debatable. I'm going to say that in the end I think that both of my authors find the California-Girls way of valuing women too intriguingly ridiculous for us to consider seriously banishing it from our culture.

Let me emphasize before I go any further in this chapter that feminism is more important to me than it is to either Ariosto or Calvino. Calvino—to tell the Absolute Truth about him—never has any real interest in feminism. Ariosto, on the other hand, would seem to . . . but his frequent radical-feminist declarations

30—HUMILITY'S DECEIT

(such as one we'll be looking at in a little while that begins "Women have always proved the equal of men in every single art in which they have tried their hand") are really just a tease for his readers, particularly for his women readers. He is not really concerned with the practical problems women have faced in the past and continue to face now in their struggle to be as free as they can.

But so what if feminism is not as important to Calvino and Ariosto as it is to me?? Who cares? Let's just get started.

A SOMEWHAT TRADITIONAL SCHOLARLY DECLARATION OF SOLEMN INTENTION
(necessary because the chapter gets kind of long and I don't want you to lose sight of its meticulously controlled basic structure)

In the first part of this chapter, I will study the "male feminist" aspects of Ariosto and Calvino. Like more than a few male humanities professors today who on the surface would seem religiously sympathetic to feminism, both authors, on the surface, show complete sympathy for women's reasonable demands that men start once and for all learning how to deal with them rationally.

In Ariosto, it seems quite natural to look at all of the *Furioso*'s women characters together and analyze the system the poet fits them into. Looking at an identical system in Calvino seems less natural. But the thing is this: I'm reading Calvino as if all his novels taken together form a single all-inclusive "hyper-novel." (Kind of treating his 10 or so *real* novels the way the ten fake novels are treated in *If on a winter's night a traveler*.)

The logic behind my approaching all of Calvino's novels as if they were all part of a single unit is provided in the discussion of a related topic in Calvino's last book, *Palomar*:

> Uno legge in età matura un libro importante per lui, che gli fa dire: "come potevo vivere senza averlo letto!" e anche: "che peccato che non l'ho letto da giovane!" Ebbene queste affermazioni non hanno molto senso, soprattutto la seconda, perché dal momento che lui ha letto quel libro, la sua vita diventa la vita di uno che ha letto quel libro, e poco importa che l'abbia letto presto o tardi, perché anche la vita precedente alla lettura ora assume una forma segnata da quella lettura.

(A person reads at an advanced age a book that is important for her, one that makes her say: "how could I possibly have lived without having read it!" and also "Such a drag I didn't read it when I was young." But yet these statements don't make very much sense, especially the second one, because as soon as she's read that book, a person's life becomes the life of one who's read that book and what does it matter if she reads it early or late, because even her life before she read it now takes on a form outlined by that reading.)

I don't wholly understand the thought. But it seems interesting and it's one I want to keep thinking about. For now, I'm sure I can apply this idea to Calvino's own fictional production in supposing that each new work changes the way we read all of his novels taken together. And of course the underlying point that I am forcing here is that you can see the Calvino novels taken together as equal to the *Orlando Furioso*.

The second section of this chapter is the part where we examine the Beach Boy attitude toward women that neither of our two authors is very good at hiding or controlling on many occasions. Typical earnest "male feminist" professors (me for example) nowadays refuse to admit that we talk feminism to women students mostly because we crave acknowledgement of our rare intelligence and uncommon sensitivity to women . . . as well as gratification of our enormous egos. Ariosto and Calvino show how the male ego and our tragic need of identity confirmations from as many women as possible make it impossible for us to even begin to relate to women in a rational way.

(Which you may find either depressing or reassuring somehow. Or both. Or neither.)

(But it's not as if Ariosto and Calvino are soft-core pornographers or something just because—as we're going to see—they use the swimsuit issue of *Sports Illustrated* as a reference in many of their descriptions of women. I mean . . . we do have to keep in mind that writing and reading about female body parts in texts made out of words is not quite the same as looking at the cover woman on Cosmopolitan or the quick flashes of evening-gowned women on Michelob by-night commercials. Even though it's not entirely different either. But let's remember throughout this whole book that we're talkin' the two smartest authors in the long literary history of The Most Sophisticated Civilization and Literary Tradition Known to Man (i.e. to those not fooled by johnny-come-lately developments in French or German philosophy or literature from the 17th century on).

And I furthermore certainly hope you don't think I'm going to imply that my two authors could have or should have been nicer to women. Cause it's obvious that labeling male writers or even not-feminist-enough women authors and filmmakers (like Erica Jong and Lina Wertmuller) as bad guys or traitor gals is unfair and boring . . .

Oh . . . I forgot, sure, sure: we all need our enemies to be sure of who we are. Me especially: you know, my traditional professor-types enemies! So women have my blessing to go on all they want blaming all their problems on men and our impossible-to-shake control of literature and television and everything else.

PART ONE

Women in the Narrative Structure

Let's start with Ariosto. At the beginning. Women are usually at the beginning of fiction. A real story can't really begin until the woman appears and announces herself at one and the same time ready for conquest and impossible to conquer. Brigid O' Shaughnessy, in the *Maltese Falcon*, for example, is my all-time favorite. What a dame! (as they used to say).

This is why the *Orlando Furioso* starts with the word "women" and ends its first line with the word "loves":

> Le donne i cavalieri le armi gli amori
> le cortesie, le audaci imprese io canto
>
> (Women, knights, arms, loves
> chivalric acts, tough-guy missions I sing . . .)

It's traditional women and traditional love interests that make literature, films, tv programs and college classes interesting. Astonishing (or stupid), isn't it . . . how endless our fascination with love connections: whether real or tragically missed or impossible?

(And who knows why? Does it even have to do with some kind of biology joke?)

But let's move on to the second stanza. In which Ariosto starts in right away on how in his own "personal" life his very own girlfriend is eating away at his tiny brain. So much so that his obsession with her makes him fear a complete deterioration of his brain-cell functioning that would make it impossible for him to finish the long poem he wants to write:

> se da colei che tal quasi m'ha fatto
> che 'l poco ingegno ad or ad or mi lima
>
> (She's drives me) almost as stark raving mad (as Orlando's going to get in this poem of mine) and if she doesn't stop wasting away my tiny mind (I might not be able to hang in there and finish this thing.)

These lines also give us our first exposure to Ariosto's partly sincere and partly phony way of talking about himself: a problem that I'll be much too interested in throughout. For now, let's just note in these first two stanzas how important women and male obsessions with them are.

We can now go on to view the outward, ornamental system of feminism of the *Orlando Furioso* that I spoke about a minute ago. It's a system that works as follows: Every time we meet a woman with depressingly traditional negative characteristics, we meet soon afterwards a positive female character—almost always a more important one—who's outgrown the kind of behavior that makes life so difficult for men.

The first canto of the *Orlando Furioso* features Angelica and Bradamante (both of whom, not coincidentally, you who have read Calvino are already quite well-acquainted with).

Angelica—absolutely and positively negative and traditional woman—is stuck in a tent some men have been holding her prisoner in. She decides to make her escape and flee to freedom in the forest of traditional female deceptions.

(Let me explain that as traditional-deceiver woman Angelica is Frigid O'Shaughnessy, an obscure-object of desire type who will never be captured by the hero. This is of course because we can never return to the bliss enjoyed at our Mother's breast [or on Dad's lap where we sucked expressed mother's milk from a bottle nippled with the natural-shape NUK brand] and that's why we're all—men and women indifferently—such selfish, impossible-to-deal-with assholes).

But near the end of the first canto we meet Bradamante, a new kind of nontraditional woman. Bradamante shows her prowess by unhorsing the Arab knight Sacripante, dumping him right out of the saddle of power. She throws him to the ground in abject humiliation right after we heard him turning over in his mind the usual lurid justifications so many of us males use to psych ourselves up for kissing or raping a women who won't admit to herself she has no reason not to be sexually interested in us.

What happens here in the first canto of the *Orlando Furioso* will be reinforced neatly by what happens in the narrative structure as a whole as it unfolds over 46 complicated cantos in which 365 distinct episodes are narrated.

For just when we've lost interest in Angelica in Canto 19 (because who wants to read any more about a woman who has been "drilled" (as current slang now has it, I hear) by Medoro, who, although he's as beautiful as you saw last chapter on page 19 or somewhere around there, happens to be a mere low class Arab who specializes of course in rather vile terrorism), Ariosto brings in Marfisa, his other main feminist character, in order to reinforce the ornamental feminist point made in Canto 1: old woman is on the way out and new woman is here to replace her.

Hence the first out-and-out feminist manifesto of Ariosto's poem comes at the beginning of Canto 20. And as the narration continues to unfold in this very, very long work, the pattern becomes clearer and clearer: by the time the two feminist heroines Bradamante and Marfisa join together in canto 37 and succeed in defeating Margannorre and the woman-hating male mentality he represents, they are clearly established as by far the most important women characters in the poem. And so they remain until the long poem finally ends.

But let's make a quick diagram of all the important women characters in the *Orlando Furioso* and how we know who they are by observing who they are paired with. In Ariosto and Calvino's fiction you can only tell who someone is by knowing who she or he is not: Ariosto's Bradamante is not Angelica and Calvino's Ludmilla is not Lotaria, for example.

But here's the chart I've thought up. I'll explain it starting a few pages down the road:

"Checking Out Some College Girls"—35

FEMALE PAIR	PLACEMENT	MEANING
ANGELICA/ BRADAMANTE	Canto 1–2	OLD WOMAN/ NEW WOMAN
Melissa/ Bradamante	Canto 3	good mother /daughter
Dalinda/Ginevra	Canto 4–6	false/true (type f)
Alcina/Logistilla	Canto 6–8	false/true (type t)
Angelica/Olimpia	Canto 8–11	false/true (type t)
Melissa/ Bradamante	Canto 13	evil mother/good daugh. (Brad's subjective view)
Doralice/Isabella	Canto 13–14	false/true (type f)
Orrigilla/Lucina	Canto 17–18	false/true (type t)
ANGELICA/ MARFISA	Canto 18–19	OLD WOMAN/ NEW WOMAN
Gabrina/Marfisa	Canto 21–22	false/true (type t)
Angelica/Isabella	Canto 23	false true/(type t)
Marfisa/Doralice	Canto 27	unnatural/natural
Doralice/Isabella	Canto 28–29	false/true (type t)
MARFISA/ BRADAMANTE	Canto 30–38	unnatural/natural
Lidia/Bradamante	Canto 34	false/true (type f)
Woman/Fiordiligi	Canto 42	false/true (type t)
Beatrice/ Bradamante	Canto 44–45	bad mother/ good daughter

Before discussing this chart, I should say that pairing opposite types is not the only way to make Ariosto's women make sense.

Another kind of geometric chart to make would be a "love triangle chart" to show how consistently women are fought over by men (or themselves fight for men). But don't worry at all about the various kinds of unfriendly objections to the chart that enemy Ariosto professors would make if I presented it at some Major Conventional Literary Conference where some dud(e) who wanted to show who's who in Official Literary Studies today was just waiting to stand up after I read my paper and tear it and me to pieces.

(So many sicky bastards always out to get you in this profession, I can't believe it. And so many people who are *so* super paranoid. And man . . . if there are any students reading this thinking of getting into this game, forget it, DON'T!! Make other plans quick. Sell cars. Sell Insurance. Anything but having to sell phony originality and insights that all sorts of fools who somehow (who knows how?) got into power are just waiting to scoff at you for. As if any of them had any ground to stand on to criticize anybody. On what grounds, huh? Because of some long-forgotten mediocre book? Or because of a book or a couple of books that *should* be forgotten as soon as possible? Or because they got their foot in the door before it got competitive?)

But where was I? Oh yeah . . . at a quick glance, the table shows how important Bradamante is at the beginning and ending of the *Furioso* and how similarly important Marfisa and Isabella are in the poem's outward feminist structure. But the most important purpose of this table is to show how all female characters have either a good or bad "essence" by comparison to other female characters. No woman has any autonomy as a complex individual who might be good and bad at the same time.

But of course, it so happens that even though many of us give lip service to the idea that all individuals are complex and unique—in our actual conversations with ourselves we very often reduce complexly contradictory individuals to some sort of good or bad essence. A typical enemy-of-the-feminists male professor for example might think to himself: "this feminist woman colleague is a complete bitch whose mediocre publications have gone to her head; that indifferent-to-feminism woman colleague is a solid scholar; this woman student has been reading too much feminist nonsense about Reuniting with Mommy's Lost Body; that one on the contrary is learning how to be faithful to the text in a professionally responsible manner . . ." and other such simplistic reductions.

(But please note that everyone—me especially—has just as prejudicial ways as that of reducing complex human beings with complex problems to positive and negative stereotypes. Yes—sorry to disappoint you—I'm very capable of thinking in negative stereotypes as I walk past young urban blacks working terrorist purse-snatching operations out of every single El station and supermarket in my neighborhood in Chicago. No, not reading anything is not necessarily a better answer than reading too much.)

Another thing the chart also shows is that most stories have to do with the truth and falseness of women—in love stories or sex stories. Pretty much every time there's a major woman character, there's always a love interest or a sex interest. Except in the case of Marfisa in Ariosto and (later for Lotaria for Calvino) for reasons we'll examine.

But now it's time to explain my chart and its categories in their personal meaning for me:

Old (Traditional) Woman//New Woman

In my opinion, the two basic questions anyone interested in promoting or rejecting feminism might want to ask (and answer in her or his own terms) are:

1. What is a traditional woman like?
2. How must a non-traditional "new woman" be different from a traditional woman?

Here's how I personally answer the questions.

1. A traditional woman is a woman who accepts existence as the object of men's desire, a thing to be fought over and won by the best man, a symbol (not a person) whose value is all on the outside, for whom external appearance is the main thing that matters, one who cannot conceive of significant self-fulfillment outside of marrying and mothering. However much she tries to pretend she can.

(This bus poster I was seeing a while back emphasizes the importance of marriage for women and for women only: it says that the odds are almost zilch that a never married 35-year old woman will ever bag a stud.)

2. Non-traditional "new woman," is different from traditional woman because she is a subject rather than an object. She conceives of her destiny, like men do, as something she makes entirely independently of her relations with lovers. She is someone who chooses and actively pursues lovers rather than waiting to be chosen. She is a person who values herself mostly for what's on the inside and has a strong independent sense of identity with no essential need of marriage and/or children. As a matter of principle, she could never ever follow a husband to a new city in which he was offered a job and she wasn't. There's just too much at stake.

False Vs. True

Men's fear and mistrust of women is so extreme that we are always ready in our mind to call them all whores. Accordingly, my false/true category is divided into two very closely related types. Type "t" is one an objective observer (if objective observers could exist) would say really has been false in her dealings with a man. Someone who's been actively and maliciously manipulative or treacherous. Type "f" is one who objectively has done nothing really wrong but one who has become a type t in the paranoid male mind.

Natural Women and Unnatural Women

Well, natural women look and act the way it seems proper for women to look and act and unnatural ones don't. But the big questions are:

1. How do we arrive at ideas of what is "natural" and what is "unnatural" for women (and men)?
2. Should we try to fight against ideas about naturalness and unnaturalness and perhaps reject some or all such ideas, even at the risk of disconcerting people we don't really want to disconcert? Or should we try as best we can to conform to what society seems to deem natural for men and women so that everyone in our family and in our society can be comfortable with us?

And the answers are, respectively:

1. We learn from Mom, Dad, Walt Disney, and Oprah.
2. No. Yes.

One Other Thing to Note

Bradamante is especially important so I want to point out one more thing about her. Bradamante is paired first with a mother figure, Melissa, and later with her real mother. This reminds us probably that if a woman wants to be a new woman she might have an especially difficult relationship with her mother.

(Another reason we learn so much about Bradamante is that she is a made-up ancestress of the Este family that Ariosto works for and praises extravagantly... as we—or maybe me with myself if you never get there—will see in Chaps. 4 and 5)

(It is interesting to note that Ariosto praises the Este family greatly even though he doesn't get paid very much by either Ippolito d'Este, or Alfonso D'Este—the co-rulers of Ferrara he works for at different times. Interestingly enough, his rather meager salary is just about as woefully inadequate as my Assistant Prof's pay today at Loyola of Chicago, one of the lower paying Universities, I think.)

The time has now come to give examples of the types of women I've been talking about.

So let's start with the Old Woman/New Woman contrast that Ariosto introduces so clearly in canto I.

Angelica, the traditional woman is desired by all the knights we meet in Canto I: Ferraù, Sacripante, and Rinaldo. She is not really described in Canto I (except implicitly in the comparison to a perfect rose in stanza 42–43), but we learn about how desirable she is by all the men chasing her all over the canto. Sacripante, for example, has crossed all of Asia and Europe just to follow her:

> Appresso ove il Sol cade, per suo amore
> venuto era dal capo d'Oriente;
> ché seppe in India con suo gran dolore,
> come ella Orlando seguitò in Ponente
>
> (His love for Angelica brought him all the way
> from where the sun rises on the world to where it sets:
> 'Cause somebody in India made him sad and blue
> When he told how she followed Orlando on a Westward
> [move.)

It is clear that the fact that she has followed Orlando enhances her desirability. In fact, her main activity is to flee in fear her many lovers:

> Fugge tra selve, spaventose e scure
> per lochi inabitati, ermi e selvaggi
>
> (She flees through forests, so scary and so dark
> passing through places too deserted, too lonely, and too
> [stark]

Angelica knows men desire her and she, like all traditional women, needs to use her power over them to play them for saps: to get them to fight battles for her instead of fighting them all herself. Here Ariosto describes how Angelica manipulates Sacripante and how devious she is:

> ma alcuna finzione, alcuno inganno
> di tenerlo in speranza ordisce e trama
> tanto ch'al suo bisogno se ne serva,
> poi torni all'uso suo duro e proterva
>
> (But some fakery or other, some trick
> to keep this fool's hopes up she slyly devises:
> so that as long as she needs him he'll be of good use
> after which she'll go back to her usual nasty abuse)

Men can never live at peace with traditional woman because they know that treachery and selfish coldness are part of her very nature. Anytime she makes sweet eyes today, we know it's only a false promise, that tomorrow she will be cold as ice just to watch the way our egos crumble.

Bradamante is the positive to correspond to Angelica's negative. She is not at all a passive object who flees, but an active subject who seeks:

> Ecco pel bosco un cavallier venire
> il cui sembiante è d'uom gagliardo e fiero
>
> (Here in the woods a knight is coming
> with the look of a man who's solid and tough)

The fact that you can't tell from her external appearance that she isn't a man is really important. Could that be one of the main points in thinking about New Woman? Shouldn't we men learn somehow to mentally place a knight's metal armor over the outward form of all the women we relate to and learn to pretend they're men?

(You know what I was thinking? I was thinking that if wives and husbands were assigned by computer to everyone who wanted one at age 27, say, and we didn't have to worry our whole stupid life about who pleased us and whom our presence affected sexually, women could walk down the street or into one of us male professors' offices and we could look at them and relate to some of them with the same relaxed spontaneity we have in relating to some of our male students.)

Bradamante shows that she is as strong as a man when she thwarts powerful Sacripante's pig-rape of Angelica. She is New Woman taking care of feminist business. Canto I ends on a triumphantly feminist major chord and the music continues and continues throughout the *Orlando Furioso*.

All the presentations of false and true women teach us to drop our traditional ideas about women and how much they love to mess up men's minds. A good early example is Dalinda in Canto 4.

Dalinda is a smart woman who has made the usual foolish choice of a man, and become an utter fool for love of Polinesso whose very name "Mr. Multitrix" should certainly have tipped her off. Although Dalinda is not aware of Polinesso's plot to demoralize Ariodante and seems somewhat innocent, it is incredibly stupid of her to agree to dress up as Ginevra and make love to Polinesso on the balcony. We forget that she is not an actively treacherous type like Angelica. Here is the sexy description of her embrace with Polinesso:

> A prima giunta io gli getto le braccia
> al collo, ch'io non penso esser veduta;
> lo bacio in bocca e per tutta la faccia,
> come far soglio ad ogni sua venuta.
> Egli più del usato si procaccia
> d'accarezzarmi, e la sua fraude aiuta.
> Quell'altro al rio spettacolo condutto,
> misero sta lontano, e vede il tutto.

> (I get there and I throw my arms wildly around
> his neck, and I'm sure no one's looking;
> I kiss his mouth and kiss all over his face
> just like I always do anytime we're together.
> More sexy than usual, he seems really turned on
> as he strokes and fondles me: oh how it suits his foul plan!
> The other guy who's watching the whole dirty set-up
> stands there, blown away, —as he sees the whole thing.)

Lurcanio voyeurs Dalinda's hot sex with Polinesso and has the typical male negative "what-did-you-expect-from-a-woman" reaction when he witnesses a woman he thinks is his brother Ariodante's girlfriend Ginevra giving all her sweet love to Polinesso.

And Ginevra? Well, she is a strong and true woman who is too easily taken by Lurcanio for a weak and false one. We are sure she is strong and true when we read about her perfect love for Ariodante:

> L'amar che dunque ella facea colui
> con cor sincero e con perfetta fede
>
> (All her love and all her devotion she gave him
> With such a pure heart and a faith oh so true)

Ginevra is every bit as true to Ariodante as he is to her. It's only Ariodante's credulity in too readily accepting his jerky brother's women-hating generalizations which leads him almost to suicide. (But don't worry: this little story, like most of them in Ariosto, has a happy ending.)

But let's move on.

With his Doralice/Isabella pair, Ariosto highlights another thing men greatly fear in women: fickleness. Doralice is the most important fickle woman character in the poem. Promised to Rodomonte, a character who needs to get rejected anyway for reasons we will overemphasize in Chapter 5, Doralice is too easily wooed and won by Mandricardo:

> poi con risposte più benigne molto
> a mostrarsegli affabile e cortese,
> e non negargli di fermar nel volto
> talor le luci di pietade accese

> (then she answers him with a lot more kindness
> and shows him her sweetness and her charms
> and she even starts looking at his face
> with eyes turned on by pity for all his pains)

Even though she does dump her boyfriend Rodomonte, I've decided to not call Doralice an actively treacherous type. A girl should have a right to change her mind for whatever reason . . . in my opinion.

(Don't we aging male professors, for example, have every right to dump our wives for our very favorite female graduate—or even undergraduate—student?)

Isabella, in contrast to Doralice, is unshakably constant, resisting all advances, ready to be faithful to Zerbino unto death. Odious Odorico—just as in love (or compulsively obsessed with sex) as Mandricardo—has no luck at all when he puts his big moves on. Refusing to take no for an answer—like a lot of men in the *Furioso* as well as on campus dates in the 1980s—he tries to rape Isabella. But in feminist refusal to submit to Odorico, Isabella kicks, scratches, and bites the asshole, shouting all the while:

> io mi difesi con piedi e con mano
> et adopra'vi sin al'ugne e il morso:
> pela'gli il mento, e gli graffiai la pelle.
> con stridi che n'andavano alle stelle.
>
> (I defended myself with my feet and hands
> and I used my nails and my enraged teeth all that I could:
> I peeled flesh off his chin and scratched up his skin.
> Screaming and yelling in anger to the stars above.)

But let's move on to Lidia. Men have never tolerated the idea that an unattached woman (and not only an unattached one) has a right to say "no thanks" to a reasonably good-looking guy's pleas for dirty love. Lidia is condemned to Hell just because she said no:

> qui dal giudicio altissimo di Dio
> al fumo eternamente condannata,
> per esser stata al fido amante mio,
> mentre io vissi, spiacevole ed ingrata.
> D'altre infinite è questa grotta piena
> poste per simil fallo in simil pena.

> (here God Himself with His Highest and Final Judgment
> damns me after death to eternally choke on smoke,
> for having been nasty when I rejected,
> while I lived, that true loving man of mine.
> This cave is full of such women: many more than I can tell
> for the same crime rotting in the same way here in Hell)

This male-revenge fantasy punishment of all the women who have rejected them highlights man's eternal fear of the "irrationality" of women who refuse them for no logical reason they can figure out. The story of Bradamante's constancy in the cantos surrounding the interview with Lidia is the positive counterweight:

> posso di lui ben lamentarmi,
> ma non d'amar Ruggiero posso ritrarmi
>
> (I can complain and complain of him as much as I want
> But don't ask me not to love Ruggiero: I simply cannot!)

But enough on old women and new women. Let's turn to the natural and unnatural ones.

Here we must contrast Marfisa's unnatural refusal to become anyone's lover with Doralice's desire to please every male who needs it so bad. Like many women back in the '70s, Marfisa almost never puts on a skirt:

> e ben che veder raro si solea
> senza l'osbergo e gli altri buoni arnesi,
> pur quel dí se li trasse; e come donna
> a prieghi lor lasciò vedersi in gonna
>
> (And even though it was truly rare for you to see her
> without her armor and the other fine tools of her warrior's [trade,
> that day she got rid of them; and just like a woman
> as the men were urging, she let everyone check her out in a [skirt)

There is something very unnatural about Marfisa. Doralice, by contrast, accepts the fact that women are "pleasure machines" to "bang on" to use an expression Bruce Springsteen once used to give us insight into the way pinball machines are just like women (and I should note in awe that he came up with a rhyme as brilliant as the stunningly natural ones Ariosto so often comes up with in his Italian: "pleasure machines" rhymed with "unsnap their jeans"):

And so Doralice's inconstancy, a fault, perhaps, is perhaps excusable if we think of how important her natural acceptance of sex is. I'll explain when we get to Calvino's Ludmilla and Lotaria what exactly is "wrong" with Marfisa.

But now I feel like hurrying up and summarizing what I've said so far about Ariosto. Think some more yourself about naturalness and unnaturalness in women (or men) and we'll get back to it a little later.

The second stanza of introduction to Canto 20—that I have already alluded to twice—is the best example of Ariosto's official feminist voice. It serves as a perfect commentary on the ornamental feminist system in the whole poem. Here it is, finally:

> Le donne son venute in eccellenza
> di ciascun'arte ove hanno posto cura
> e qualunque all'istorie abbia avvertenza,
> ne sente ancor la fama non oscura.
> Se 'l mondo n'è gran tempo stato senza,
> non però sempre il mal influsso dura;
> e forse ascosi han lor debiti onori
> l'invidia e il non saper degli scrittori

> (Woman have gone straight to the top of the heap
> In every field in which they've tried to succeed.
> And anybody who is aware of what's told in many stories
> Has heard what they've done in both the present and the
>   [past.
> But if the world is not used to hearing this kind of story:
> Let's not let the maleficent influence last a minute longer:
> Because we know now just what women can do and how 'til now they've been held back
> Only because of the foul envy and the ignorance of male
>   [writers.)

Now, if you go back again to my stupid chart, you can again see how important Bradamante and Marfisa are in supporting Ariosto's feminism. And in canto 37, it so happens, Marfisa replaces Margannorre's old Male Law with a New Woman's Law:

> Quivi s'indugiar tanto, che Marfisa
> fe' por la legge sua ne la colonna,
> contraria a quella che già v'era incisa
> a morte et ignomina d'ogni donna.
>
> (Here they took some time out, enough for Marfisa
> to have *her* laws written on the column,
> laws contrary to the ones carved there before
> calling for the ignominious death of every woman.)

This description of Margannorre's law as a set of statutes that exists for the "death and ignominy" of women makes it clear what's at stake. Professors trying to sell feminism want us to believe that "normal" life under a patriarchy that despises women often leads to the death of a woman's spirit. Marfisa abolishes Margannorre's law and provides his kingdom with new laws under which new women like her can start flourishing and very soon lead infinite other women to prosper in the same way.

But no more. Enough on Ariosto's feminism for the moment. For before we turn to Ariosto's California-girl descriptions and Calvino's too, let's look a little at what Calvino's structures are like. No, I don't mean how long and fat his penis was when erect or how round his buttocks were. That's still not really an important factor in evaluating a male. What I'm going to be talking about is how he sticks women characters—in his books.

But before I lay my Calvino's women chart on you, check out a quick listing of all his books and of the years they first came out. I place these books in meaningless categories just for the sake of the chart. And to make it interesting for anyone who knows the real names of Calvino's novels, I've given each of them a stupid-English-pun title.

CHAPTER TWO CHART TWO
WHAT DID CALVINO WRITE AND WHEN?

PHASE OF CAREER	TITLE OF NOVEL	DATE
Youthful Realistic	Cry of The Spiderbaby	1947
Classical Traditional	The Count Splits	1951
Classical Traditional	Barren Treeson	1955
Classical Traditional	Dream (K)nights	1959
Mature Realistic	Pure Smog	1959
Mature Realistic	A Party Watchman	1963
Mature Realistic	Wildmark in the City	1963
Experimental (SJF)	Cosmiconjob	1965
Experimental (SJF)	Tease-Zero	1967
Experimental (TF)	Double-Crosses of Destiny	1969
Experimental (WCF)	IC MindCities	1972
Late Experimental	If a (K)night	1979
LaterExperimental	PallorMarred	1983

CHAPTER TWO CHART ONE REPEAT
CALVINO'S WOMEN

CHARACTERS	WHERE FROM	MESSAGE
Rina/Pamela	S-baby/Splits	False/true (f)
Sister/Viola	Treeson	False/true (t)
PRISCILLA/BRADAMANTE	(K)night I	New/old woman
Ursula/Ms. Vhd^2	Conjob	False/true (t)
Jenny/Zylphia	Tease	False/true (f)
Angelica/Bradamante	Double Cross	New/Old woman
Lotaria/Ludmilla	(K)night II	New natch/old un
Bather/Mrs. Palomar	Pallor	Who knows?

What this chart shows is this:

1. Limitations Like in Ariosto

   Here again women characters inevitably wind up in categories in which men (or male authors or voyeurs) worry about understanding them, relating to them and winning their love. Women can't exist outside of relations with men or outside of men thinking about them.

2. Serious Feminist Concern

   In Calvino's fiction, we can discern (or make up) a carefully controlled progression in which our author duplicates Ariosto's careful balancing of discouraging female negatives with heartening female positives. There are two major phases to note.

   (a) Phase One: Triply Correcting Rina

   Positive Pamela in *Splits* starts the correction of disastrously negative Rina from *S-boy*. But it is the hint of Bradamante in Viola (in *Tree*) and the actual rebirth of Bradamante in *K(night)I* that convincingly completes the correction—at a very important turning point in Calvino's career: when, in the mood of the 1960's, he decides to become a freespirit and challenge the traditions and traps of conventional fiction.

   (Oh I forgot. I don't really believe in turning points and shifts and moves to different types of fiction in Calvino's career. My book is supposed to be about how all his books fit smoothly together in an utterly phaseless unity.)

   (b) Phase Two: Latter Fictive Feminism

   After the Pamela-Viola-Bradamante triple play in the 1950's, Calvino keeps on pairing positive women with negative ones in his freaked-out Mid-Sixties Science-Is-A-Joke Fiction (the two books by Calvino I don't particularly care for). But in *Double Crosses* he affirms feminist principles emphatically in order to prepare for a culminating treatment of women in *(K)night II* a book very closely related via Ariosto—to*(K)night I*—as you can see from its title.

In *Double Crosses*, Bradamante appears again. (We can see her as the key character who unifies all of Calvino's fiction in just the same way she does in Ariosto. But why am I always in such a hurry to simplify things so drastically?)

In *Double Crosses*, I was saying, Bradamante makes only a brief appearance but it's a very significant one in my story because in it she punishes a very typical man for seducing and abandoning a typical young woman. This brief appearance of Bradamante in the role of avenger helps us understand better Bradamante's finale performance in *(K)night II* as Ludmilla, the female reader. In this book, in fact, we get not only Bradamante but also a precise clone of Marfisa—in Lotaria.

Ludmilla-Bradamante and Lotaria-Marfisa are two different kinds of New Women with different ways of refusing to play men's games. Ludmilla-Bradamante, Calvino's dream of a perfect reader, is an assertive person with her own tastes and her own interests. But she understands that she cannot fully pursue those tastes and interests without humoring men on occasion and entering into relationships with them.

But my quoteless commentary on the chart is getting boring. So we'd better start in with the quotes. And oh yeah: in this chapter I'm sometimes going to quote Calvino as if he wrote poetry in stanza form instead of just regular everyday prose. This is to call attention to the fact that he selects and arranges words just as carefully as a poet like Ariosto does.

Calvino begins his first novel with a nasty reference to a treacherous woman. The word "women" is not exactly word one on page one of novel one like in Ariosto, but it's close. Very early on we hear an insult about Rina directed at Pin—her young adolescent bother, I mean brother: "tu e quel materasso di tua sorella." ("You and that mattress of a sister of yours).

(This is Calvino's equivalent of Ariosto's page one reminder that men's desire for women is the best example of the foolishness of all brain-rotting desires. We men insanely try to make mattresses out of women—when it is much more sensible to make women out of mattresses—by masturbating away our dreadfully predictable fantasies.)

In *Spiderbaby*, we only learn about Rina through Pin and his older friend Cousin's reactions to her. Rina has no voice (I mean typographical characters) to contradict Cousin, a real jerk of a woman-hater who says things like:

> "Lo sapete perché continuano a prendere dei nostri? Perché c'è pieno di donne che fanno la spia, le mogli che denunciano i mariti, tutte le nostre donne ora che vi parlo sulle ginocchia dei fascisti che gli lucidano le armi per venirci ad ammazzare."

> ("Know why they keep on coming and grabbing our guys? On account of all these fucking women who spill the beans, wives who hand over their husbands to the police, all our women who right now while I'm rappin' to you dudes are at the fascists' knees shining up the weapons they're gonna use when they come blow us away.")

We can understand that we ought not to take Cousin's opinions very seriously. (His opinions about everything are as thoroughly wrongheaded as mine, for example, or maybe some of yours.)

And yet . . . the novel doesn't show us very much what's wrong with Cousin's ideas about women, by—for example—showing some active partisan women machine-gunning Nazi heads off.

But in his second novel, Calvino starts to make up for letting women down so much in his first one. With Pamela, he gets the ball rolling and shows us an independent woman's point of view. Here's how Pamela tells Medardo's Bad-Half how she'll only enter into a relationship with him on *her* terms:

> Voi volete tenermi lì prigioniera e poi magari farmi bruciare dall'incendio o rodere dai topi. No, no. V'ho detto: sarò vostra se lo volete ma qui sugli aghi di pino.

> (You, Milord, wish to keep me prisoner over there in your castle and who knows maybe even have me burned by fire or gnawed at by rats. Forget it! I've told you: I'll be yours if I have to be but only out here on the pine needles.)

And in his third novel—*Treeboy*—we meet Viola, my favorite Calvino woman, a great horsewoman:

> Gli Ombrosotti, quando la vedevano galoppare a briglia sciolta, il viso quasi immerso nella criniera bianca del cavallo, sapevano che correva a un convegno col Barone.
>
> (The Ombrosots, when they would see Viola galloping with free rein, her face almost buried in the white mane of her horse, knew that she was racing to a meeting with the Baron.)

Like Bradamante, she is free and self-moving, riding hard and tough through the forest of life and doing things her way. (To get an idea of her independence, think of a woman biker nowadays busting along at 80 miles an hour on a big motorcycle on the Interstate with her long hair flowing wild to the wind.)

But let's meet Calvino's Bradamante herself:

> Ora sono fianco a fianco
> Rambaldo e il cavaliere sconosciuto
> Questi va sempre mulinando la lancia
> Dei due nemici, uno tenta una finta . . .
> Ma il cavaliere pervinca in quel momento appende
> la lancia al gancio della resta e dà mano allo stocco.
> Si lancia sull'infedele: duellano.
>
> (Here they are side by side
> Rambaldo and the unknown knight
> who's whirling his lance around and around.
> As for the two foes: one tries a feint . . .
> But the unknown knight in purple at that very moment
>   [hangs up
> his lance on the hook of his rest and takes out his bludgeon.
> He flings himself on the Infidel: they duel.)

In this first description, we of course have no idea at all that Bradamante is not a man. And you can see how active she is as a warrior in this Battle of Chapter Four—where she is by far the most impressive knight in the combat action. Here Bradamante rescues Rambo—I mean Rambaldo—from two nasty terrorist-type

Arabs. And as you would expect, she does everything much better than any man around her.

But before we leave Calvino's three hit novels from the 50's, let's get some laughs from the negative traditional women we meet in *Treeboy* and *(K)nite I* just to note how Calvino imitates Ariosto's good-and-bad-women games. Or just to shake our heads at how unfair some of ways we laugh at women are.

In *Treeboy* we've got sicky Battista and her sicky private kitchen jokes:

> Ma dove metteva le mani lei non si sapeva che sorprese mai potessero arrivarci in tavola: certi crostini di paté, aveva preparato una volta finissimi a dire il vero, di fegato di topo e non ce l'aveva detto che quando li avevamo mangiati e trovati buoni.

> (But wherever she laid her hands you never knew what surprises might turn up at the table: certain paté crostini, she once prepared for us—extremely subtle in taste to tell the truth—made out of mouse livers and she hadn't told us except after we had eaten them and found them excellent.)

Battista is the victim of a hypocritical society that has forced her to put on a nun's clothing for the rest of her life because of some trivial youthful sexual adventuring. But there's something about her delight in making fools of men that reminds us how much we men fear women's power over us.

Priscilla in *(K)night I* is the fearfully insatiable man-eater type:

> Questa degli orsi è tutta una trappola
> E' lei stessa che li alleva,
> per farsi liberare dai più valenti cavalieri
> che passano sulla strada maestra
> e attirarli al castello
> ad alimentare la sua insaziabile lascivia

> (This business with the bears is all a big trap:
> *She's* the one who raises them,
> to get the most valiant knights to come and free her
> anytime they happen to pass by on Main Street

from where she can entice them to her castle
to feed her insatiable lasciviousness)

Calvino is playing Priscilla's negative against Bradamante's positive. It's a pretty bad negative, to be sure. But it all just seems a big farce when all-too-fleshy Priscilla meets her match in non-existent Agilulfo (the heroic knight who is all armor and no body, a perfect image of an author or a professor).

In *Double Crosses*, we meet Ariosto's Angelica herself. She appears in the story of Orlando Crazed for Love that I'll be checking out at too great length in my next excuse for a chapter:

la figura di questa donna bionda
che in mezzo alle lame affilate e
alle piastre di ferro
affaccia l'inafferrabile sorriso di un gioco sensuale
noi riconoscemmo Angelica

(the figure of this blond lady
who even with sharpened blades all around
and amid the iron coats of armor
plays her sensual game as she flashes her unattainable
                                                                                      [smile
we recognized as none other than Angelica)

But if we have Angelica in *Double Crosses*, we know that Bradamante has to be somewhere near at hand to correct her. And as we read or re-read *Double Crosses*, in fact, we sooner or later figure out that Bradamante's the one we had met in the very first story of the collection: "La storia dell'ingrato punito" ("The story of the male ingrate who got just what all men deserve"). Here, first we meet a woman, then we later meet an unknown warrior whose face is completely concealed.

An unknown warrior whose face is hidden under her visor? Of course! It can be none other than Bradamante in disguise!

This version of Bradamante in *Double Crosses* is the scorned woman we had suffered with early in the story who returns to settle old scores with men by...

(Wait just a minute: you know—it just now occurs to me that I forgot to explain why my Calvino-women chart skips *Nonsense Cities*, a book he wrote describing imaginary cities that all have women's names. Well ... it's a book I like quite a bit but frankly one I don't understand too well.)

(But if I must—let me offer one isolated observation that might be relevant to this chapter. Maybe we can look at some of the invented cities as "Cities of Angelica" and others as "Cities of Bradamante." The quintessential City of Angelica would be "Zobeide" "the trap city," last and worst of the five cities of stupid human desire, a city in which men chase in vain their dream of raping nude Angelica. And the quintessential City of Bradamante might be "Eutropia," perfect in its position as middle among cities of exchange, an "ambiguous miracle," just like Bradamante. In "Eutropia," an impossible need is met: the need for all things to change (like women for their own good) and yet at the same time remain in their same comfortingly traditional place (like women for their own good.)

In *(K)night II* we're on much firmer ground. (I think). Ludmilla-Bradamante, like in Ariosto, is no game-player in dealings with men. As soon as her fictional fiction-reading partner starts in with his boring male paranoia-hysteria routines, she cuts him off abruptly:

> "Io e tanti altri!
> "Cos'è? Una scena di gelosia?"
> "E che diritto avrei?"
> "Credi che a un certo punto potresti averne diritto? Se è così, è meglio non cominciare neppure."
> "Cominciare cosa?"
>
> ("Me and everybody else!"
> "What the fuck is this? A jealous number?"
> "Shit ... I forgot ... what right do I have?"
> "So you get the idea someday you're going to have that right? Is that it? If so, Mr. Right, let's not even start."
> "Start what?")

Ludmilla-Bradamante has no interest in the kind of jealousy games Angelica types derive their desirability = identity from. She wants to approach a love story in as straightforward a manner as possible. Ludmilla is this way also in her "relationships" with the jealous male author-teachers she gets involved with. Like a sensibly independent woman in a love relationship who takes her pleasure without investing her whole soul, Ludmilla takes pleasure out of books without prostituting her mind to the author's. It so happens that each of the ten "novels within the novel" of *(K)night II* fails to satisfy her and she rejects them one after the other. She even literally rejects Silas Flannery, Calvino himself, when he makes some laughably lame sexual advances towards her.

(I know you want me to quote you the scene. Well—I'm going to give it in a later chapter. Stick around if you don't have anything better to do.)

Lotaria-Marfisa is also a creator-of-her-own destiny who knows how to make her own personal choices. Thing is, though, she makes choices that are extreme. Silas-Calvino in his diary disapprovingly compares her with Ludmilla:

> "Luckily I can check out through my binoculars that other woman reading and reassure myself that not all readers are like that bitch Lotaria."

What he dislikes in Lotaria is the tedious tenDensiticity of her aridly intellectual way of reading his books. She is the unnatural reader who is becoming a wrong kind of new woman: one who can't avoid excess compensation and remember that one can be gentle and subtle and still be independent.

(But I must acknowledge that it may well be that all readers are equally tendentious and tedious. *I*, for example, am both of those things in the way I highlight similarities and suppress differences between Ariosto and Calvino.)

(And one more thing I should say. It could be that Calvino doesn't mean for us to take his repudiation of Lotaria as the "voice of good sense." It could be that Silas's "voice" (I mean "typographical characters") comes out of the mouth of an aging paranoid author who simply can't face the frightful reality of the reader's absolute freedom to make whatever she wants out of whatever she reads.)

But whether or not Calvino is directly repudiating (or indirectly de-repudiating) aridly intellectual critics who distort literature in order to have things to say in their stupid class lectures and to publish in Important (to whom?) Books with Brand Name Designer Scholarly Publishers—we don't necessarily have to accuse him of openly attacking women and their just aspirations for new and different treatment.

Maybe he's just being a boring liberal who's proposing a moderate, human feminism in which women acquire new virtues without losing their traditional sensitivity to others that we men—who can't relate at all to one another—so greatly envy in them.

(Though, come to think of it, frankly, I personally haven't seen that much genuine sensitivity in the women I've met in my life. They're all so fucking self-absorbed—in different ways at different ages, of course. But it's all the same: they're never REALLY interested in MY problems or MY ideas.)

So we finally come to understand how new women can be new without sacrificing the best qualities of traditional women (or the best qualities traditional women have traditionally appeared to have until you get to know them better). Bradamante and Ludmilla assert themselves without sacrificing the basic affability and sweetness that are so infinitely pleasing—whether phony or not-in traditional women.

PART TWO

Kissing Feminism Good-Bye

In the second part of this chapter, we've got to look closely at another kind of structure. The structure of women's bodies. And what do we see? The same story you see any time you turn on the t.v. or stand with ferocious impatience in front of the magazine covers that are supposed to take your mind off the intolerably slow supermarket check-out line.

What we see (I mean read) in Ariosto and Calvino is the anatomy of the impossibility of significant improvement in relations between men and women.

Ariosto and Calvino both keep the squeezing hand (or eye) of male stupidity firmly placed on certain arbitrary lumps of flesh on certain parts of women's bodies. For even though Ariosto and Calvino dress some of their women in feminist clothes—neither author ever forgets to fantasize about what it might be like to feel up the secret parts of women's naked bodies.

Because if Ariosto and Calvino really wanted us to learn to accept new values in our relations with women, wouldn't they need to teach us to look a little differently at women's bodies?

Because if you're a man the thing is this. Once you start longing for women's bodies, don't you get trapped in a fearful system in which you can only look at complex human beings deserving of complex respect as objects to be longed for?

But any time they describe women, Ariosto and Calvino have no qualms about Beach-Boying out. They reassure their male readers—and their women readers who get into being looked over—that it's o.k. to be a regular guy.

Which we all knew anyway, didn't we? Because isn't any man who tries to be something more than a regular guy in looking at women, a man lacking in natural male vitality?

But it's time now for a pause.

Because with those two questions that I frankly have no idea how to even start answering, we've gotten to the most important part of this chapter.

But before I get into the heart of (phony) darkness in this chapter, I want to take a breather and make a preliminary remark to convince you that Ariosto and Calvino are undermining their explicit and implicit feminist rhetoric on purpose.

This somewhat long preliminary remark is one I want you to feel extremely free to skip.

An Extremely Skippable Preliminary Remark:

In speaking about Ariosto in this book I have not yet mentioned that some of the main things I am saying about the *Furioso*'s women could not be as said of the 1516 or the 1521 version. So let me say that: Some of the main things I am saying about Ariosto's treatment of women could not be said of the 1516 or the 1521 version.

The 1516 or the 1521 version? Yes, the 1532 version is a longer version (6 more cantos, 46 in all) in which Olimpia (part of whose body we will soon be looking over) is introduced and in which Bradamante's role becomes clearly defined. I waited till now to tell you about the 3 editions of the *Furioso* because I didn't want to load you down with too much info about a work you'll never read.

(Don't worry about it though. There are so many videos of great films one can now easily rent—even at 7–11 stores for just two dollars or sometimes even a dollar. So I'm really serious about not wanting you to worry about not having time to read Ariosto. Unless you, like me, like to worry stupidly about books you haven't read and won't ever have time for. Hey: I'm not being facetious at all. Really I'm not.)

(But remember: enough people in Italy will always be forced to read Ariosto. He'll never be forgotten. I mean, since they have a lot of repulsive snob ideas over there about the tremendous importance of Great Books. Ideas we're currently working on outgrowing over here on this side of the Atlantic. And I'm not being facetious in this remark either! Read this book carefully and you'll understand that, dammit!)

But where was I in this skippable preliminary remark? Oh yes. I was telling you that Ariosto's game with feminism is only played out to its full extent in the carefully revised last version of the *Furioso*.

And it is also true that we can't understand Calvino's undermining of feminism without a look at *(K)night II* and *Pallor*. Which if we want to (and I want desperately to) we can think of

"Checking Out Some College Girls"—59

as books that make us rethink the way we read everything Calvino ever wrote.
Preliminary Remark Over. Start of WOW FINISH on next page.

So let's look at a description which appears for the first time in the 1532 version of *(K)night Fury*. A description of Olimpia. She's all nude on a hard rock. (Not in a hard rock cafe, mind you, just on a hard rock) And it's just after Orlando, (in an imitation of a Saturday-morning cartoon featuring robot heroes or superman, or he-man or the like) has showed up at the last possible moment to rescue her from the Woman-Devouring Sea Monster (That Stands For The Patriarchy).

(I just know you're interested in more information about my almost seven-year old's cartoon watching habits. So here it is: his favorite male heroes of the moment are (1) Marshall Brave-Starr, the black indian sheriff of New Texas and (2) Optimus Prime, Leader of the Autobots. He watches these cartoons after school and absorbs their messages with the same strangely rapt awe you can observe in professors like me reading scholarly books in a university library.)

In stanza 59 of Canto 11, before the official description begins we already get turned on by a description of how nude Olimpia fails when she tries to hide the three prize female parts with the only two dainty hands the jokester of a Lord gave her.

But the real description begins in stanza 67. It consists of Five Full stanzas in which the male author lingers over Olimpia from top to bottom. Fair man that he is, (or order-and-symmetry-crazed poet that he is), Ariosto splits the description right down the middle: 2.5 stanzas for her face, neck and shoulders and 2.5 stanzas for the pornographic turn-on parts. If breasts are your thing, I'm sure you'll be interested in checking out the following stanza:

> vinceano di candor le nievi intatte
> et eran più ch'avorio a toccar molli:
> le poppe ritondette parean latte
> che fuor dei giunchi allora allora tolli.
> Spazio fra lor tal discendea, qual fatte
> esser veggia fra piccolini colli
> l'ombrose valli in sua stagione amene,
> che 'l verno abbia di nieve allora piene

> (They were a lot whiter than untouched snowdrifts
> and were much softer to the touch than ivory,
> those round little breasts of hers seemed like milk
> you've just now squeezed out from a cow.

There was a space between them going down just like
the kind you might see between cute little hills
in their shadowy valleys—so beautiful in the season
when the winter has made them all snowy FULL.)

Here, the breasts of Olimpia are described as all snowy white and rounded smoothness, a perfect purity ready to be defiled by the impure male eye and male touch. And note the hot reference to "squeezing" the milk out of the nipples of a mother cow with all them soft sexy liquid double l and m and n sounds in sleazy sexy Italian that roll pornographically on one's tongue, like in words like "molli" (soft) and tolli ("you squeeze out"). And the whole thing is wrapped up with *the* key word in breast adoration: FULL.

After this description, heated up and turned-on so much by his (even if purely) verbal fantasy lick-over of Olimpia's non-existent body, panting Ariosto is sure she's even hotter looking than Venus herself (the goddess of love from that dippy 50's song) and more perfect than a composite statue some Togaed Greek made while observing the best parts of a whole pack of fine Greek (sorority sister) nudewomen at a wild 1980's fraternity party featuring a dog that looks as close to Spuds McKenzie as the boys can come up with.

The thing is—we men again and again get into fantasizing a perfect hole surrounded by the best parts of all the women we've ever known (to paraphrase Julio Iglesias and Willie Nelson but let's not forget Paul Simon's nice song *Kodachrome* about all the girls he knew when he was single that he dreamed of putting together for one night) when we want to get ourselves really turned on.

(In Ariosto's text, Oberto gets to live out our collective fantasy when Olimpia is handed over to him by Orlando, her rescuer.)

Olimpia is one of the new women on the chart? One who is contrasted with Angelica because she is forceful and assertive? At the level of narrative structure, yes. But at the level of bodily structure? Not at all.

(Hey I like the joke, don't worry if I run it into the ground. This is my book and I can show as poor taste as I want—so many young academics are so into showing off their sophistication and aristocratic taste that they produce utterly lifeless stuff—which the Big Names they're trying to impress can't really respect anyway—on account of the Big Guys' inevitable absurd paranoia that the new young guy or gal might be more "brilliant" than they were in their long-lost prime, more of a "genius.")

(But consider this: do you think that if the vague words "brilliant" and "genius" didn't exist to obsess the twisted academic mind then professors would be freed from their rivalries? Can you imagine what freedom there would be if we all really admitted we were all equally stupid no matter what self-flattering books we wrote in order to prove to ourselves and a few friends we sort of respect that we're among the few in the "grade-A" mind club in a world of B and C mind-level professors.)

(Don't get me wrong: I personally make no claims at all to anything but an "F" as my final grade for overall mind-level. I'm totally free of such absurd worries.)

(And don't get me wrong: I see no real need for us professors' silly hatred of each other to end. We all know we have to hate at least a few selected each others in order to write and teach with proper professional passion. It's God's revenge on people who try too hard to figure out Her mysterious ways.)

But what I was starting to say was that it could well be that feminism in Ariosto is just a put on. Check out this line:

Ella è gagliarda ed è più bella molto

(She's robust and oh so pretty)

This is the first line to tell us the truth about Bradamante being a woman and not a man as we'd supposed. But it also tells the eternal truth of how women always will be perceived in our culture.

(No, I'm not being serious in saying "always will be." I admit I have no idea what the future will be like just because I've read a few overrated books among the trillions which have been produced. I'm not the sort of professor with some mediocre pet theory who walks around the sunless dark university corridors with this look on my face as if I was sure I knew something. Or do you get the idea I'm precisely that kind in my own annoying way?)

Well, o.k.: whether or not "Ella è gagliarda ed è più bella molto" tells the eternal story of women in our culture, at least it helps me tell my story of what women are most important for in Ariosto and Calvino.

After he gets the fact of Bradamante's strength out of the way, Ariosto lingers lovingly over her beauty, giving us in fact a very short preview version of passages such as the Olimpia description: a preview of a body-part connoisseur's pleasure, that is here the pleasure of pronouncing the lip-licking letter "l" and a pair of ecstatic "o" sounds: "bel-la - mol-to.

(Now you know why Italian men so greatly enjoy saying "ciao bella" to women they pass on the street. Although—watch out for them: rapes have been somewhat on the increase over there of late, like the Piazza Navona rape of March 8th, 1988.)

Don't worry, it reassures the male reader, however strong certain women are, whatever they do on the battlefield (of Academia, say) we won't have to grow up and start thinking beyond visual enjoyment and fantasy conquest. And who cares if our fantasy needs have to ruin or severely limit so very many of our relationships with real-life women? Sure, a few women can do their just-like-men—or why not?—better-than-men routines. Geraldine Ferraro can intellectually outclass blustering George Bush in their 1984 debate, (even if anti-intellectual American newspapers didn't seem to notice) but nothing really has to change.

And so even though Ariosto respects Bradamante by never fantasizing what she might look like nude, he doesn't take her all that seriously as an independent character. Go and read for yourself how everything she does, she does for her lover boy Ruggiero. She knows preparation for marriage and motherhood is what her, after all, traditional story has to be all about.

(And you know, Ruggiero isn't nearly good enough for Bradamante. Anytime he gets near a women who is willing to fuck him or he thinks owes him that overrated favor—he forgets Bradamante instantly.)

And things aren't a bit different with Calvino's Bradamante. After she has saved Ramb(ald)o from the usual nasty Arab terrorist types (as usual described with scorn according to absurd prejudices of European culture), Bradamante is described in a long, lingering paragraph which begins and ends as follows:

> Rambaldo non credeva ai suoi occhi.
> Perché quella nudità era di donna:
> un liscio ventre piumato d'oro,
> e tonde natiche di rosa,
>
> e tese lunghe gambe di fanciulla.
> . . . e si mise tranquilla ed altera a far pipì.

> Era una donna di armoniose lune,
> di piuma tenera e di fiotto gentile.
> Rambaldo ne fu tosto innamorato
>
> (Rambaldo did not believe his eyes.
> Because the nudity he saw was a woman's:
> a smooth belly plumed of gold,
> and round buttocks of pink
> and stretched out long maiden's legs
> ... and she began calmly and proudly to go pee-pee.
> She was a woman who had harmonious moons
> of tender feather and of gentle flow
> Rambo was instantly in love.)

So here we have the checking out of Bradamante's ass which Ariosto had withheld from us. Calvino knows, though, that he's carrying out something Ariosto implied. We knew she had to be as hot-looking and as perfect as Cybill Shepherd shot through a cheese cloth in "Moonlighting."

But in Calvino, this is all nontraditional isn't it? Demystifying? Liberating us from tradition? Making fun of falling in love in literature?

'Cause instead of falling in love at first sight with her angelic face, Rambaldo falls in love with Bradamante when he checks out her fine golden pubic hair while she is squatting during a piss. And how many romantic heroines having you seen or read about pissing or taking a shit lately?

But let's not kid ourselves. Calvino is still playing the same game. This revelation-of-the-warrior-woman scene shows how Calvino, like Ariosto, is not at all interested in thinking seriously about how we can start to learn to really respect women for their non-physical attributes.

But at this point I've got to ask a series of questions about how (and whether) men's way of looking at women and relating to them can or should change. I've put off asking some basic questions until now because I wanted you to get used to my way of approaching certain questions so that you would become better able to think for yourself about whether I'm asking the right questions or not. Here they are: Are we correct in assuming that women need a (at least relatively) rational world in which—as happens for men—they are more respected for their achievements than they are prized for how they can make themselves look? And if a certain kind of traditional physical beauty and sexiness does have to remain at least a little important (does it?), don't we have to make it just as important for men—for whom it's not really fatal to be hopelessly unhandsome and misshapen, is it? I mean we know it's nice for a guy to be cute. But is it really important for us to be attractive to women in the way someone like—who knows?—Brooke Shields is to men?

(And that reminds me . . . Brooke Shields is still in college at Princeton, isn't she? Or has she graduated already? Doesn't she take Romance Languages? Isn't she the kind of student that gets really into all things "Euro," the kind that will take Italian and Italian lit courses as an even more ultimately elite snob experience than French? My gosh: why didn't she come to Loyola of Chicago?—as I've told you—we've got a rich kid's party center in Rome she could have even gone to hang out at and party and jet to other European capitals from. Why she have to go and go to Princeton for?)

Enough questions. Back to Ariosto and Calvino and tradition. What we need to talk about now is not how the new women characters contrast with the old young women characters but how they actually remain old women beneath their new-woman outward disguise.

There aren't really any new women at all. Woman are "right" in Calvino and Ariosto only if they are properly good-looking and made-to-love and to fondle (or dream of fondling) dirtily.

Let's check out Calvino's treatment of women in *Conjob*. Then afterwards I'll tell you why I chose that book in particular.

Let me now play for you another Calvino-women triplet: three titillating little numbers in a row with no commercials to interrupt your straightforward swelling pleasure (if your a man) or your 'our-bodies-are-the wondrous-crown-of-creation' revelling (if you're a woman):

> p. 16 e io in questo brancicare alle volte finivo per afferrare una mammella della signora Vhd Vhd, che le aveva tonde e sode, e il contatto era buono e sicuro, esercitava un'attrazione anche più forte di quella della Luna, specie se . . . riuscivo con l'altro braccio a cingerla sui fianchi.

(And in all this shuffling around sometimes I would wind up grabbing one of Mrs. Vhd-Vhd little boobs, which were round and firm, and the touch felt good and reassuring and had an even greater attraction for me than the Moon's, 'specially if I managed get my other arm around her hips.)

p. 57: La signora Ph(i)Nk$_0$—tutti i discorsi vanno sempre a finir lì ... la signora Ph(i)Nk$_0$, il suo seno, i suoi fianchi, la sua vestaglia arancione

(Mrs. Ph(i)NkO—no way I can stop my thoughts from going back to her ... Yeah: Mrs. Ph(i)NK0!: those breasts, those hips, that orange robe of hers ...)

p. 138 (già mi bastava chiudere gli occhi per vederla, (Ursula), venire avanti, in un atteggiamento che sapevo suo anche se diverso da tutti gli atteggiamenti a lei soliti: le braccia tese all'in giù aderenti ai fianchi, torcendo i polsi come se si stirasse e nello stesso tempo accennasse a un divincolamento che era anche una maniera quasi serpentina di protendersi)

(already all I had to do to see Ursula was to close my eyes. And I'd see her coming forward, in a pose that I knew was hers even though different from all her usual poses: her arms stretched downward clinging to her hips, twisting her wrists as if she were stretching and at the same time giving you a hint of wriggling that was an almost serpentine way of leaning forward.)

Yes a triple play: tits and hips, tits and hips, hips alone: grabbed stealthily, or unreachably lost in the dreamy past or impossible future in endless remembrances or fantasies. Calvino distributes these descriptions strategically throughout the whole *Conjob*. The book contains 12 stories, half of which are unhappy love stories.

This, mind you, in a book that's supposed to be some kind of "liberating" avant-garde sort of thing. A rocket launched to bust the gravity barrier of earth-bound fiction.

But why can't fiction be liberating and avant-garde in ways that at least start somehow to help rid us of stupid male fantasies and all the trouble they cause?

O.K., I know you're thinking: "HEY, LIGHTEN UP BRO': can't you see that these descriptions of women are a just little joke included by our delightfully inventive writer. Can't you see that a lot more significant things are going on in *Conjob* than the checking out of women. Leave the guy alone. Only in *one* story, the one jokingly titled "The Form of Space" do we have the start to finish voyeuristic obsession that nerdy Qwfwq has with Ursula's (Angelica's) "form in space," the hot body she is so vain about. In the other stories, Calvino's just doing a little joke—to remind us just how predictable woman's place always is in fiction.

Well granted a little. It's not impossible to lay off on the attacks on the *Conjob* . . .

But, come on! Doesn't it bother you a little? Why does Calvino find it so natural to go the soft-core-porn route to show us here as he will repeatedly later on that he can't see any way of escaping from tradition in books or even in thinking about oneself as author, teacher or less professionally messed-up type of person? Why can't he figure out some other way to anchor his stories in tradition?

Is it not in fact a fact (sisters of the jury) that he has by now resigned himself to the fact that a very traditional notion of women is somehow necessary for fiction to be understandable and pleasurable? And is it not furthermore in fact a fact that he is acknowledging perhaps that our culture in which people buy his books and force the guilt of success upon him can't even begin to shake off its astonishingly arbitrary definition of "woman"?

Why is he so proud that beside reading and understanding science books most of his science-fearing readers (given the narrowmindedness and absurd prejudices of all us literature snobs) have no courage to try to read, he can also walk confidently down the streets of fiction looking at women the way they're supposed to be looked at?

Let's go back to Ludmilla.

In Chapter 7 Calvino does well to give us a perfectly symmetrical, non sexist description of a sex act in which we are surprised when the author starts giving us Ludmilla's point of view:

> E anche tu intanto sei oggetto di lettura, o Lettore: la Lettrice ora passa in rassegna il tuo corpo come scorrendo l'indice dei capitoli, ora lo consulta come presa da curiosità rapide e precise . . . (in te) s'insinua un dubbio: che lei non stia leggendo te uno e intero come sei, ma usandoti,

usando frammenti di te staccati dal contesto per costruirsi un partner fantasmatico, conosciuto da lei sola . . .

(And meanwhile you too have now become a reading object, o Male Reader: the Female Reader is now looking over your body as if she were checking out a table of contents, consulting your body as if she were personally absorbed in certain points she was particularly curious to get more information on . . . a nasty doubt begins to form in your head: the doubt that's it not you she's reading at all—you in your oneness and wholeness—, but that she's using you, using single parts of your body taken out of context so that she can make a fantasy partner for herself, a man she alone knows.)

Women have every right to create fantasy images of men with no respect for the real man they happen to be in bed or in the elevator with. But beyond Chapter 7 *(K)night II* is not able to develop the symmetry fully. For in the other chapters, we learn that Ludmilla, presumably a normal everywoman of presumably average looks and intelligence like you (or below average looks and intelligence like me) must become a creature of fantasy fiction in the mind of both the Nonexistent Reader in the book and the real readers outside it. From Chapter 6 on, we begin to associate Ludmilla with the typical female characters = sex objects to conquer and/or abuse of male fantasy fiction: a mysteriously veiled Arabian Princess and an intriguingly masochistic woman (like the one in *Blue Velvet*) who loves being tied down in front of a computer keyboard and forced to produce third-rate scholarly books like this one at a word-processor.

In order for the cold commentary in the numbered chapters of *(K)night II* to become a story it has to make its main woman character into a traditional woman character, into Angelica.

Maybe I should say here that *K(night) II* is much less interested in talking about women and sex than it is about readers and reading. Bradamante-Ludmilla has to be a perfect kind of—at heart—traditional woman only because she represents the perfect reader as perfect woman: mysterious, unpredictable, uncontrollable, and maddeningly unconquerable to be sure, but also warm and sensitive enough on occasion to enrich a male author or a teacher's life by acknowledging to some extent his male cleverness.

And even though she has to ultimately reject him and his teachings the way women always reject too Desperately Earnest And Sensitive males, a woman like Ludmilla knows that rejection is just what male authors and teachers need if they are to go on writing and teaching and feeling deliciously unloved and unappreciated.

So there's really no hope at all. When you listen carefully to the background voices in "California girls," you keep hearing the high voices go: "girls, girls, girls I dig the girls girls girls." There's just something about stories that makes it impossible for people like me and maybe you to feel comfortable with a story without a traditional woman/fantasy girl in an at least sort of traditional place.

So things pretty (much) . . . stay . . . just as they are—even though not exactly entirely . . . which is of course both absolutely awful but also absolutely reassuring as well. Although maybe not really.

I wish sometimes my relationships with my (SIC!) women students could be different than the way they are. Not all the time maybe but sometimes.

Oh but who knows what male professors want these days?

But, reader, space is running out for this chapter, so I have to leave entirely to you the problem of figuring out sex-relations stuff in a much much more interesting way and figuring out whether you want to bother asking yourself personally:

1. Just where are we now, anyway?
2. Where do we need to go and what are the commercials like over there?

Yes, it's very late and my late-model ironic word-processor is showing:

Document: 1 Page: 69 Line: Not Funny Position: Missionary

❧

CHAPTER THREE

LAUGHING AT THE WRITER-BOY'S MADNESS

I. Some Comments About Methods and Madness

By now I'm sure you professor types reading this book not really meant for you or anybody else think you got this book all figured out. You think that in each chapter I'm going to start with something that only applies to Ariosto and force-feed it on Calvino. Guess again!

This chapter it's Calvino's influence on Ariosto we're talkin'.

Yeah, yeah, yeah . . . another trite, worn-out, overdone trick, I know, I know. I guess I was born twenty or thirty years too late—hey I can't help it . . . But screw you if you think you can laugh in judgment of me. Reread your own stuff and then try and argue seriously that it gives you authority and license to attack another sensitive human being for her or his stupidity. Or if you who haven't written anything—(no big deal at all but romanticizing or overrating silence could very well be a mistake, too)—think about how full of imperfections upon imperfections your writings would be.

Anyway, if you (whatever kind of reader you actually are) really want it, I got plenty of justifications I can give for looking upside down at this crazy question of being under the traditional influence when it comes to madness. So let me explain a little.

The thing is this. I mean—a Well-Informed General Reader of Calvino might assume that the Orlando character who goes nuts is somebody that Calvino takes over from Ariosto. Because it's obvious in *Castle of Destinies* that Professor Calvino is grabbing most of his important characters directly off the List of the Top-Ten-Way-Too-Often-Written-or-Taught-About Characters from Literature (Faustus, Parsifal, Hamlet, Lear, Macbeth).

But the story of where Orlando comes from is more complicated than that.

By the time Ariosto decides to write a put-on of Chivalric literature with Orlando as his title character, this 400-year-old legendary hero has already long since become a standard generic-brand masculine hero. (You know what I mean: hunk of big muscles, man of Few but Essential words or grunts—John Wayne or Sylvester Stallone say—who belongs to no author in particular.)

(And of course in talking masculine hero types I'm also talking about the kind that a typical young male literature academic such as myself identifies with in his fantasies of conquest of Highest Honors in Academia and/or spiritual (yes, yes only spiritual in the abstaining age of AIDS) conquest or at least one good-looking, bright, highly sensitive, absurdly enthusiastic innocent co-ed or young grad student per academic year.

(The kind not yet disenchanted with men and their astonishing boringness, the kind whose shy, blushing eyes you can make say "how wise and learned you are when you quote intriguing foreign texts with such seemingly authentic accents" "how sensitive and vulnerable you are when you shake your head and talk about the absurdity of human desire" "how so so so you are you are you are" etc. etc.)

And so when Ariosto (making fun of Milton's seriousness) says he's going to say things about Orlando "unheard nor in prose nor in rhyme," he knows very well there's nothing new to say about this kind of character. Male hero types and their madnesses or bitternesses when life doesn't give them just what they were sure they wanted before they found out that's all it was are always the same. So there's no reason we shouldn't suppose Calvino comes first.

And one more thing. If I wasn't so interested in this book in pairing everything for the sake of a certain kind of conceptual clarity the need for which I hope to outgrow soon (Ariosto/Calvino; Renaissance/modern; man/woman; oppressed traditional real women/non-oppressed untraditional unreal women so far in this book, truth/untruth; optimism/pessimism author/character, coming up), this chapter could have plenty to say about Cervantes' re-writing of Ariosto's rewriting of Calvino in Chapter 26 of the first part of *Don Quixote*. But Cervantes is a problem I'll leave for you to work out for yourself.

(Literature Academics always waste so many pages and pages just to satisfy mindless production requirements. They ramble on and on and on tediously and overstate their cases to the point of absurdity. Often recycling the same "devastating insights into life," saying pretty much the same exact boring thing in article after article, book after book, dull class after dull class.)

(But of course people in power always blame subordinates when things don't go right so it's always the students who get blamed by academics for not being sophisticated or as intellectually curious as kids were before eight hours a day of tv became somehow obligatory.)

How admirable my restraint in not writing about Cervantes in this age of excruciatingly well-read Comp Lit snobs! You know (or may know) the type: the ones who are so proud of being able to leap across seas and jump east and west and north and south across certain continents (ignoring others) from one paragraph to the next of their essays and awe-inspiring class lectures before mouth-agape students! I'm extremely proud of myself for holding off on my comments about Cervantes.

But if you've read Cervantes, keep in mind that you might very well think of him from time to time during this chapter. And, come to think of it, next chapter too: there's going to be this incredibly Cervantean (or Don Quixotean) quote from Ariosto about how enchanters and enchantresses abound in our midst and about how they create all sorts of problems in our strange minds. But let's get back to. . . wherever it is we were.

II. Calvino's Original

This is the first Orlando-goes-mad tale of 'em all. Which of course it really is for the many people in the world who read "The Castle of Crossed Destinies" before opening the *Furioso* or the *Quijote*.

****

Calvino's tale of "Orlando Crazed On Account of Love" is the fifth tale in the first half of *Destinies*, the first of the two consecutive stories that will later be imitated by Ariosto. And let's remember that the card-game in this book is this: certain people who have lost their voices are sitting around a restaurant table on top of which there's a deck of tarot cards and they figure out that they can tell their life stories by laying out sequences of tarot cards.

"Laughing at the Writer-Boy's Madness"—73

Now the tarot "Tale of Orlando" is the climactic tale in the first half of this cloven-in-two book. (The first half is entitled "The Castle of Crossed Destinies" and the second half is "The Tavern of Crossed Destinies"). This first half that (as we've seen in the last chapter) begins with a story featuring a Bradamante clone climaxes with the orgasmic eruption of Orlando's madness.

Orlando goes mad on account of love when Angelica rejects him by choosing Medoro. But of course it's not only frustrated erotic desire that's at issue. Orlando's disastrous experience with obsessive sexual love reminds us of the catastrophic results all desires lead to.

(This, I should note, is an important point made in most literary works. Or at least in most literary texts typically recommended by four out of five 1980's intellectual heavyweights, or pseudo-heavyweights which nowadays is exactly the same thing since who can judge whether the technical language in most books and articles written by intellectuals today means anything at all.)

(By heavyweight I mean someone who can drop hot and heavy big names of French, German and once in a while Italian or Spanish philosophers or literary critics that they have not really understood more than superficially. Or—o. k.—even if maybe they might have understood the Big Names and Just Why They're So Crucial better than I can manage it's not as if they ever show that the Names have ideas more interesting or less banal than yours or mine.)

But—as I was saying before I allowed my insecurities and paranoia to fly me completely out of control . . . it is very important to keep in mind that in Calvino and later on in Ariosto, the character of Orlando is associated with the author at his nudest self. The Orlando tale in the first half of *Destinies* is in more or less the same position as the tale in the second half in which Calvino emphasizes his own madness and inability to understand himself and his wars with beasts inside and outside himself. (This is the tale entitled "anch'io cerco di dire la mia" ["I too give it a shot at saying what I have to say"].)

Whereas the Orlando story is about how the beast within explodes and rages against the desire-denying world outside, Calvino's "personal" tale reminds us of the rage pent-up and ready to explode in writers in general and in academic writers in particular who attack each other with such desperate vehemence.

74—HUMILITY'S DECEIT

In our story, Calvino tells the story of Orlando in a style which will influence Ariosto tremendously. Ariosto demonstrates the futurity of Calvino by retelling the story in a style and tone identical to the style of the original hit from the late 1960s.

(Yet another reminder of what great goodness there used to be in those already ancient times!)

In his original tale of Orlando, Calvino emphasizes that Orlando is completely out of harmony with nature. The hero will go mad in a woodland setting where he discovers that the previously virgin Angelica has had wild sex with Medoro, the effeminate Arab pretty boy with earrings and dyed, punk-rocker blond hair you met in Chapter One.

Orlando's realm is the solid masculine realm of war and he is warned by the Talking Heads of the trees of the feminine forest of love not to desert the battlefield:

> "Perché diserti i metallici campi di guerra
> regno del discontinuo e del distinto
> le congeniali carneficine
> in cui eccelle il tuo talento
> nello scomporre e nell'escludere?"
>
> ("Why desert the heavy metal fields of war,
> reign of the discontinuous and the distinct
> the sublime slaughters where
> your talent excels in undoing and excluding?")

Calvino's style here is characterized by use of flashy pairs of nouns, verbs and adjectives. With a show-offy pair of intellectual nouns referring to the reign "of the discontinuous and of the distinct," for example, Calvino sets the stage for the contrasting, equally slick description of the reign of the continuous. Orlando may be victorious on the field of war but the forest of love will utterly defeat him:

> nell'umido fondo del bosco femminile c'è un tempio di Eros
> dove contano altri valori
>
> (In the moist depth of the female forest there is a temple of Eros where you need other kinds of skills.)

This slick metaphorical characterization of a rain-drenched forest as a moist vagina covered by pubic hair again underscores how important the masculine/feminine contrast (in which the feminine must be somehow incomprehensible and obscurely and irrationally menacing and fearful) is for writing and thinking about the world. (Again and again and again and again we are reminded in Calvino and Ariosto that if the traditional distinction between the basic male and female opposition were to disappear, thinking and writing as we know them probably would become impossible.)

As it turns out, Orlando's experience in the female forest leads him to a thoroughly negative understanding.

Physically inverted, hanging upside down, Orlando tells us that the only way to accept the world is to learn to read it backwards:

> Lasciatemi così. Ho fatto tutto il giro e ho capito. Il mondo si legge all'incontrario."
>
> (Leave me like this (upside down). I've been there and come back and now I see. You have to read the world backwards.")

But as he tells of how Orlando (like all ardent desirers) goes mad, Calvino puts the story of desire into interesting perspective by pressing hard and heavy on the irony pedal. For example, the moment that Calvino describes Orlando's losing his mind, he floors the pedal completely.

Actually there are two different irony pedals beneath Calvino's steering column:

> 1. The direct ironic reaction pedal: phony comments about the author's own gut sympathy for Orlando's pitiable plight.
> 2. The flashy literary style pedal.

Direct Reaction

Calvino emphasizes his own very very personal horror just when Orlando is completely losing control:

76—HUMILITY'S DECEIT

> Io chiusi gli occhi. Non mi reggeva il petto alla vista di quel fiore della cavalleria trasformato in una cieca esplosione tellurica pari a un ciclone o a un terremoto
>
> (I closed my eyes. I could not stomach the sight of that flower of chivalry transformed into a blind explosion of force equal to a cyclone or an earthquake.)

And soon after, he tells us how he personally "regrets" and "deplores" Orlando's inactive sword and the hero's wasteful expenditures of energy:

> ... rimpiansi l'ozio della Durlindana rimasta appesa a un albero e dimenticata nel *Sette di Spade*, deplorai lo spreco d'energie e di beni ...
>
> (I regretted the idleness of Orlando's sword and I deplored the waste of energies and goods ...)

Literary Style

Besides the narrator's overstated sympathies, there is the author's overstated style. The moment of madness for Orlando is a desolate moment indeed, as far as content goes, but the style reminds us that we do not read books in order to find out desolate truths about the absurdity of desire or about the inevitability of one form of madness or another and the bottom-line incomprehensibility of the world.

(These are truths we of course all have to work out for ourselves in our own ludicrous "psychic adventure" [to borrow a cute phrase I heard at a talk of some French intellectual whose name I am capable of dropping if necessary in some conversation in which I'm being a phony, but whose works seem to me at superficial glance to be made for other uses than reading].)

Calvino's text holds calmly to its irony to remind us that the author realizes that his tale is no final account of madness, no last word.

An excellent example of Calvino's irony is the description of the Matto, the tarot card which gives an idea of just what Orlando looks like in his mad state:

> Nei capelli gli restava attaccata roba d'ogni genere, piume di tordo, ricci di castagna, spini di pungitopo e grattaculo, lobrichi che succhiavano le spente cervella, funghi, muschi, galli, sepali.
>
> (All sorts of stuff got stuck to his hair: thrush feathers, chestnut husks, mouse-sting and ass-scratch thorns, earthworms that were sucking out his wasted brain, mushrooms, musks, roosters, sepals.)

This description is far more detailed than the card it is based on would warrant. The ironic style of referring to Orlando's sucked-out dead brain rebels against the lugubrious heaviosity implicit in the content and assures the reader that the author knows how much he himself is thoroughly caught up in the madness. Any desire to either get to the bottom of (or make a final statement about) madness and desire or distance oneself somehow (God knows how?) by writing or teaching others about it is ludicrous. Writing and teaching acts are clearly enough manifestations of human desire as a Colossally Stupid Problem rather than acts whose objective content could somehow point the way to solutions in real life for either writer or reader, teacher or pupil.

Yes, Calvino accepts that fact that it cannot be stated too many times that desire leads to madness and that the writer's or teacher's desire to understand the madness of the world and distance her or himself from it even somewhat are the craziest of all. In telling and retelling the story, in reading and rereading the story of madness, the marvel is renewed that no definitive pessimism can ever be put forward, no progress is possible, no history of ever-increasing ironic awareness, no greater irony piled upon irony.

III. Ariosto's Imitation

And so it is that when Ariosto finally decides he too might as well write about Orlando as anybody else, he knows that his task is to reproduce Calvino in a perfect photocopy. In stressing Orlando's battlefield valor in early passages concerning Orlando, Ariosto is careful to describe the hero's massacres (his excellence in uncomposing bodies and excluding people from life) in a way that gives us an exact equivalent of Calvino's strange characterizing of Orlando's massacres as "congenial." He emphasizes how congenially Orlando massacres by describing how the hero keeps a steady flow of assorted body parts flying through the air:

> Non pur per l'aria gemiti e querele
> ma volan braccia e spalle e capi sciolti.
>
> (Not only through the air moans and laments
> fly but arms and shoulders and severed heads as well)

Having established Orlando's mastery in the male realm of undoing and excluding (an obvious reminder of what academic writers, male and female, are always trying to do to their predecessors and rivals) and having done so in exactly the same tone as Calvino, Ariosto takes Orlando into the female forest and again describes the hero's coming apart, his own becoming expelled from the ranks of the sane.

Orlando goes into the female forest, looking for repose but getting involved in things female and incomprehensible to the male intellect (as we learn again and again and again in fiction for some reason) is never the right idea for us men:

> Quivi entrò per riposarvi in mezzo
> ed ebbe travagliato e difficile sosta
> e più che dir si possa empio soggiorno
> quell'infelice e sfortunato giorno.
>
> (Here he cruised in to get a little rest
> but got only grief and torment instead:
> and was miserable much more than I can ever say
> that so horrible and so terrible day.)

Orlando's fall in Ariosto is preannounced in exactly the same kind of flashy style he had observed in Calvino. Check out the pairs and the piling up of schmaltzy adjectives: "travagliato" e "duro" "infelice e sfortunato." Ariosto obviously remembers quite well how Calvino had made his chattily intellectual talking forest warn Orlando of impending doom.

But as Ariosto describes Orlando's gradual discovery of Angelica's treachery, he draws out the story considerably more than Calvino. Especially when he tells us at length how the hero discovers a poem written by Medoro in celebration of fine sex with Angelica. But Ariosto comments on the action in just the same way Calvino had done. At the most dramatic moments, the reader realizes that the mad, despairing author is simultaneously distant and close to his mad superhero.

Let's move the camera in for some closeups on this text you're almost certainly never going to read.

After Orlando reads Medoro's poem (a poem written in Arabic that Orlando translates for us into European Pastoral in order to make fun of the limitations of Comp Lit snobs), the hero is very near going completely mad. At this point Ariosto tells us:

> Credete a qui ne ha fatto sperimento
> questo è il duol che tutti gli altri passa
>
> (Believe somebody who's been there his share
> this pain's harder than all others to bear!)

He is protesting that he knows how it feels to be rejected by someone we're in love with. He is of course also imitating Calvino's phony despair at Orlando's plight and the plights of all victims who glory so self-pityingly in their victimage. Ariosto's "believe-me-I-been-there" statements, are, like Calvino's, always announced with an overprotesting language. He always shows he realizes that there's no complete escape from smug self-satisfaction with one's literary (or phonily anti-literary) style.

And nowhere is the overdone literary style more evident in Ariosto than in the concluding stanzas of Canto 23 in which Orlando's furious revenge on the female forest is completed more thoroughly than in Calvino. But here again Ariosto rips words shamelessly out of the soil of Calvino's book:

> e fe' il simil di querce e d'olmi vecchi,
> di faggi e d'orni e d'illici e d'abeti.
>
> (And he did the same thing to oaks and old elms,
> to beeches and birches and ashes and firs.)

The catalogue of uprooted trees is an expanded version of the catalogue in the passage-through-the-forest section in the Calvino chapter in which Calvino identifies various kinds of common trees he pretends he can see on the ten of clubs tarot:

> Orlando vi posò una carta: il Dieci di Bastoni. Vedemmo la foresta schiudersi malvolentieri all'avanzare del campione, gli aghi degli abeti farsi irti come aculei d'istrice, le querce gonfiare il torace muscoloso dei loro tronchi, i faggi svellere le radici dal suolo per contrastargli il passo

> (Orlando placed a card on the table: the ten of Tarot Clubs. We saw the forest grudgingly open herself up as the hero advanced, the needles on the firs becoming stiff like porcupine quills, the oaks swelling their muscular trunk-chests, the beeches pulling up their roots from the soil just to get in his way)

Ariosto, then, steals from Calvino in each and every phase of his version of the account of Orlando's fall into madness. He has nothing new to add to Calvino's account. But "making it new" is not the point. The point (if there can possibly be one) is to try and help us cope somewhat with the disappointments our desires lead us too. Or maybe just to self-indulgently join in on the eternal literary whining about life's limitations. Since of course we all know it's not all that bad ALL the time—don't we?

(But if you're interested in a culminating kind of whining and self-indulgence: stick around for Chapter Five.)

For now, since we're on the subject of Orlando's madness, let's go on to take a quick look at Astolpho's failed recovery of Orlando's sense of reason.

IV. Astolpho's Cure

Orlando is raging mad and can only become normal again if Astolpho goes to the moon to get Orlando's lost sanity. Ariosto follows closely Calvino's account of Astolpho's flight to the moon on the Hippogryph, but like his predecessor, is not at all serious in suggesting that it is really possible to recover one's lost senses.

Let's briefly compare the two accounts. In Calvino's original, the author describes Astolpho as "un tipo leggero come un fantino o un folletto, che ogni tanto saltava su in guizzi e in trilli" ("this guy who was light as a jockey or a little elf who would jump up every once in a while in wrigglings and trillings"), who always exudes nonchalance in his every gesture, like a Joe Piscopo character on a Miller Lite commercial. Unlike all other characters-narrators in *Castle* who carefully place the cards in their story on the tale-telling table, Astolpho sends cards flying through the air with snaps of his index finger on his thumb.

This light-hearted "fantino" or "folletto" character is not a figure to be taken seriously. And in fact, Calvino's narration of the "Storia di Astolfo sulla Luna" is by far the most openly comic tale of the *Castle* collection. For example, in a long speech, Charlemagne raps casually and off-handedly about Orlando's loss of sanity:

> "comunque sarebbe un fatto di cui non dico vantarcene ma parlarne in giro senza vergogna, magari scrollando solo un po' il capo, ma il guaio è che alla pazzia lo ha spinto Eros, dio pagano, che più è represso, più devasta"
>
> ("or anyway even though it wouldn't be a thing to be all that proud of we could at least go around talking about it without shame, you know, shaking our heads and all that, but the trouble is that it's Eros a pagan God who has driven him to madness, a God that the more you repress him, the more he lays waste.")

And Astolpho is an unreal, only-in-a-book character (even more so than typical unreal Calvino-Ariosto Made-Only-For-A-Role-In-A-Book characters) who always just happens to have what it takes to get out of impossibly difficult situations. For when he finds out he has to go to the Moon to retrieve the specially-marked vial of Orlando's lost wits, we find out about his Hippogryph:

"Astolfo il suo Ippogrifo l'aveva" ("Astolpho had his own flying Hippogryph handy")

When Astolpho lands on the moon, Calvino has him run into a poet who is intent upon "interpolare nel suo ordito le rime delle ottave" ("inserting in his web the rhymes of eight-verse stanzas"). Calvino is not specific about who he is referring to, but he imagines this poet that Astolfo runs into is someone as obsessed as he himself is with style. And also obsessed with the mad, senseless earth and with the question of how to joke about the hostile incomprehensibility of the cosmos.

As the story continues, there is in fact no recovery of Orlando's senses by Astolpho on his trip to the moon. We had learned in the Orlando tale that Orlando's lost faculty of reason was in a vial stored in "Valle delle Ragioni Perdute" ("Valley of Lost Senses of Reason"). And in fact, Astolpho is told by a hermit (a wise man or a magician) that there is a valley on the moon where "uno sterminato deposito" ("a boundless storehouse") of "storie che gli uomini non vivono" ["stories that men (feminist sic—hereafter sic fem or fem sic—whichever I feel like) never live"].

But when he's actually on the moon, Astolpho meets only this unnamed poet, the only other writer we meet in *Castle* besides Calvino himself. The unnamed poet is represented by the pen-wielding "Bagatto" tarot, the same one Calvino will use to represent himself in "I too give it a shot at telling some sort of personal story." He finds out from the writer himself that no such valley exists on the moon. "La luna è un deserto" ("The moon is a desert wasteland"), Astolpho learns, where no solutions for any problems of the "terra insensata" ("senseless earth") are to be found.

Ariosto will take all these elements and develop them somewhat further in his copy of the same story. He has obviously noted that Calvino had not named the mysterious poet on the moon and he decides to become that poet, the complete describer of the moon. So he makes a joke out of actually describing a real "Valley of Lost Senses of Reason" in very specific detail. A place where in fact Astolpho *can* recover Orlando's lost sense in a vial labeled "Wits of Orlando."

But it's only a joke. Ariosto has no more faith than Calvino in solutions to madness. We see this clearly when we pay close attention to the descriptions of Astolpho and the role given to him. For in canto 15 of the *Furioso*, Astolpho is referred to as "l'aventuroso Astolfo d'Inghilterra" ("The swashbuckling Englishman Astolpho") and as "il buono Inglese" ("The good-souled Englishman"). These epithets remind us that he is a simple good-hearted, adventure-seeking character, the egoless sort who comes around to help others, the kind who isn't in it for her or himself, the kind you find only in fiction.

In Canto 15, Astolpho's first important appearance, the Sorceress Melissa gives him a Horrible Horn, the sound of which scares beyond all imagining anyone who hears it. Astolpho also carries a "beautiful and useful" book that helps one fight enchanters and their enchantments. Later on he will receive a magic lance and take possession of Calvino's Hippogryph. Astolpho has many more miracle salvations to accomplish in Ariosto's long poem than the one salvation mission he fails to carry out in Calvino's short tale.

But he's exactly the same character nonetheless. Once, for example, he saves a group of Male Knights from the race of the Murdering Females (= certain modern feminists, not the nice, reasonable type who smile sometimes at male colleagues and male students) by blowing his magic horn.

(As if it were that simple for men to solve the problem of Feminists Who Can See Through Their Mediocrity and Cynical Male Strategems EVEN TODAY for Using the Power Society So Unfairly Gives Them to Abuse Women At Home and in the Workplace for the Sake of the So Very Fragile Penis-Guided Male Ego.)

Here is how Ariosto describes the fantasy defeat of the feminists at the hands of Astolpho who has sounded his Horrid Horn and sends all feminists in the world racing away in terrible fear:

> Di qua di là, di su di giù smarrita
> surge la turba, e di fuggir procaccia.
> Son più di mille a un tempo ad ogni uscita:
> cascano a monti, e l'una l'altra impaccia.
> In tanta calca perde altra la vita;
> da palchi e da finestre altra si schiaccia:
> più d'un braccio si rompe e d'una testa,
> di ch'altra morta, altra storpiata resta.

> (Here and there and everywhere bewildered
> the women's crowd surges and strains to get away.
> There are more than a thousand at every exit:
> Mountains of them fall down, tripping each other up.
> In such a mad rush some women lose their lives;
> others get squashed by boards or windows:
> more than one arm gets broken and more than one head too,
> some women are left dead, other women just maimed.)

When he later describes Astolpho's visit to Earthly Paradise and then to the moon, Ariosto is careful not to be serious. In Calvino, Astolpho is sent to the moon by a plain-old hermit. In Ariosto, Astolpho will happen to go up on his Hippogryph to the Earthly Paradise (The Garden of Eden) and meet Saint John the Evangelist. Saint John then takes him up to the moon to give him a complete guided grand tour.

One of the most important things that Saint John tells Astolpho is that he could never have made it back to Eden without God's assistance:

> "che né il tuo corno, né il cavallo alato
> ti valea, se da Dio non t'era dato."
>
> ("Cause your horrible horn and that wild winged horse, too wouldn't work for you, if God didn't want them to")

God is thus jokingly tied in with the magic devices that the poet uses any time he needs to come up with nick-of-time solutions (like in cartoons or westerns) at desperate moments. There is no question that in the repeated references to God in the story of Astolpho in Eden and on the Moon that Ariosto is influenced by Calvino's thorough skepticism about divine or other solutions to human problems.

Ariosto is careful to use the epithet "aventuroso" ("lucky and adventurous") in describing Astolpho during the Earthly Paradise episode to remind us that the voyage there and to the moon is light-hearted and fanciful just as it is in Calvino. Talking God seriously and thinking seriously about what He might think up in heaven of our madness down here is something of no interest to Calvino and Ariosto. Or something that their pervasive irony doesn't allow them to take seriously even if they wanted to.

V. A Few Words About Pervasive Irony

Pervasive irony? O.K. now that I'm done talking about Astolpho, it's as good a time as any to say something about Pervasive Irony. Readers who start to get into Calvino or Ariosto always, utterly without exception, unanimously agree that "Pervasive Irony" is the syndrome that best describes both authors' attitude towards life, literature, and themselves.

Both authors, for example, give us characters like Orlando and Astolpho that we can't take too seriously because they want to make sure we always keep in mind how necessary (even if often impossible) to struggle as much as we can against taking ourselves so very seriously.

With their Pervasive Irony, they are also exploring not only the limitations and predictability of literature but of life in general. It is curious that at a climactic moment in the Orlando tale written at more or less the midpoint of his career, Calvino speaks of a descent into "il cuore caotico delle cose, al punto d'intersezione di tutti gli ordini possibili" ("the chaotic heart of things, the point where all possible worlds intersect") and that near the end of the story of Astolpho he speaks of an order opposite to the one we know: "dove l'asino è re, l'uomo è quadrupede, i fanciulli governano gli anziani . . ." ("where donkeys are kings, people are four-legged, the young rule over the old") in order to protest against both fiction and life in which however much one tries to escape the limitations of a particular order in which we find ourselves living and thinking about life and its problems in a certain way, the prisons imposed by our literary and other traditions and their arbitrary logic come to trap and stifle us thoroughly: "Viene il momento che lo acchiappano e lo legano, Orlando, e gli ricacciano in gola l'intelletto rifiutato." ("The time comes when they grab Orlando and tie him up and shove back down his throat the intellect he had refused").

Orlando's problem is that he cannot avoid the stupidly predictable business of desiring and being brutally disappointed in the first place and in the second place that once he goes mad he can't just stay mad and not have to deal with the limitations of an imposed kind of rational thinking about life, literature and the self. This is fundamental to Calvino's Pervasive Irony: all stories he has to tell are forced on him by a limited system of literature that reflects also the limitations of ways of thinking about life. In *Castle*, we see how stories make us think of life as a journey (viaggio) through forests battles and bedrooms (attraverso foreste battaglie alcove) that can lead to "tesori e banchetti" ("treasures and banquets") at which we will joyously celebrate our achievement of greater self-fulfillment or greater victories than our adversaries. As if life were as simple as the Olympics or something.

There is no escape once one starts to listen to stories and to think of her own life as a story-quest in which desires and longings might somehow lead to fulfillment rather than maddening disappointment.

And yes, here too Ariosto is very attentive to Calvino's meditation. In the intro of Canto 24, Ariosto asks:

> qual è di pazzia segno più espresso
> che per altri voler perder se stesso?

> (What sign of madness clear and plainer than this
> that desiring another you fuck yourself and get so really
> [pissed?)

There is no way to put more bluntly than that how ridiculous it is to be caught up in desire for something outside the self.

And since we've been talking style this chapter, let's note the harsh rhyme in the concluding couplet between "espresso" and "se stesso" where the double "s" hisses in protest (a la Calvino) at being forced to go at least partially mad on account of desires we simply can't overcome. A moment later, Ariosto tells us that in certain lucid intervals of mind he understands just how crazy one has to be to become a lover a writer a teacher or anything else. But his attempts to bow out of the mad waltz are useless because he is infected deep down in his very genitals:

> Vorrei tosto uscir ma non posso
> Perché il male è penetrato fino all'osso.

> (I wanna get out but I just can't seem to
> 'Cause the disease has penetrated right to the bone)

෴

CHAPTER FOUR

LIES IN TELLING THE TRUTH

By this point in my book, I'm more than a little tired of my own false words. And I'm not only tired with the false words I'm using in this book, but also of the ones I'm forced to use when I speak in front of classes or with colleagues.

It's incredible how much useless expenditure of nervous anguish and waste of vital forces all our jobs demand. But please don't get the idea that I'd ever want to imply—God forbid—that dropping out and living on welfare was some kind of answer.

(But even though I'm well aware of the limitations of all our professions . . . it will be clear enough that I'd like to convince you that my peculiar profession has especially disappointing limitations—slightly more disappointing than the ones you find in competing career choices. At least that's a High Level Truth I'd very much like to affirm in a book like this . . . if it was possible to know such things. Which as we'll see for certain in this chapter it isn't at all.)

But right now what's especially important is that you look closely at the typographical characters in these chapter-opening paragraphs and note how their blurred appearance communicates to you my disaffection and boredom with this treacherous, devious and immoral business I don't remember how I got stuck in: a strange business involving cut-rate word-recycling and teaching Americans of a certain class not to worry very much about the tens of millions of people in the world who are poorer than they need to be.

(As if people like you and me could ever really learn to care about anything outside our own little worlds and our petty problems and squalid little passions!)

Well, anyway, on account of my sense of exhaustion . . . in this chapter, I'm going to let Ariosto and Calvino do almost all of the bullshitting . . . on the subject of demystification. I'm going to delight you with many quotes from both authors that demystify literature thoroughly and convince us beyond all doubt that authors and literature professors really *are* as irredeemably mad as wild Orlando to write or teach something as worthless as literature. And, what's more: to desire that people love, respect and admire us greatly for our efforts.

But let's stop being so vague about "demystification."

What we need to do is make up an arbitrary, systematic explanatory system (like Freud's, Marx's, Kate Millet's etc.) that misses pretty much all of the important points about the reality it's supposed to describe. Actually—we have to start out by defining "mystification" and then count out one by one the ways that literature covers up the truth with thick mists.

Well, if we freely adapt a randomly chosen dictionary definition of the word "mystification" to our literary purposes, we can come up with a formulation like: *literary mystifiers are writers, teachers or intellectuals that support the hoax that literature teaches us Important Things About Life by slyly playing on the vanity, stupidity, credulity or inexperience of their readers or students.*

(Now of course one thing that has to cross your mind is that this very book you are reading or skimming somehow supports the hoax that literature is important. Or maybe you're mistakenly reading this book for a course in which you have to write a paper on Calvino and you still remember how on the first day of class they passed out a sheet that told you Five or More Reasons Only Absolute Fools Scorn Literature—and it hasn't ever occurred to you that an Official University Document written by a committee of veteran professors might be mere propaganda from a Devious Special-interest Group (hereafter abbreviated as "DesPig") ... But the plain fact is—that every book (especially this one) about literature (and nowadays almost all very serious literary works themselves) is written by someone who tragically yearns for one or more of the following:

1. job security in an increasingly hostile world in which everyone is always knifing everyone in the back for increasingly hard-to-fathom reasons
2. a promotion for more money for self-indulgent trips abroad and irrational book-buying sprees
3. a chance at a better job in a better city or better country with better weather where the people remember better how to live life better.

4. a longer list of publications for his or her resumé and next public introduction as a "scholar or author with a staggering, even mind-numbing quantity and range of publications attesting to her (his) intellectual vigor and fearless search for the truth etc. etc."
(But I just can't help adding that sometimes I'm almost sure that true intellectual vigor and dedication to the Real Truth might very well entail leaving the Academic Profession because-precisely—it's a profession with so many flatter-your-co-workers and flatter-yourself rituals (in resumés, etc) that we professors really do lose sight of our True Limitations—no matter how much we try to pretend we understand them clearly.)
5. greater self respect as an intellectual and greater certainty of being above the general common herd of excruciatingly mediocre college professors—multitudes of whom even the Best Brand Name Institutions somehow get stuck with.

(But wait a minute! Why am I letting myself get all worked up? The only point I needed to make here is that the large number of books people write about literature in our culture do not prove anything at all—about whether or not literature is important in helping us better understand ourselves and the world.)

(To put it another way: demystifiers of literature hold that ideas about life you get from the best literary works are in no way superior to competing ideas in current circulation (in America, say) about what life is for and how it ought to be lived: ideas about Having It All shown on Michelob commercials, ideas about how intolerable it is to settle for second place expressed by athletes and sports commentators, ideas about how the quality of life just might depend on the quality of your investments on brokerage-house commercials.)

But let's get back to literary mystification and make up three distinct (but interrelated) kinds of mystificatory hoaxes people who read too many books can't avoid getting caught up in: (1) the Usable Character Hoax (2) the Literary Wise Saying Hoax (3) the Authorial Attitude Hoax.

I. The U. C. Hoax

When we read literary works, we usually, like Dante, divide characters into (a.) good ones that make good decisions about how to live life and (b.) bad ones that make bad decisions. The U. C. Hoax is that to some extent we can learn to imitate good characters and to avoid imitating the evil ones in our own lives.

(Or maybe even pick a single good/bad character—Sam Spade, say—to imitate. Remember the incredible "I'm not gonna play the sap for you" speech Spade somehow manages to deliver to Brigid O' Shaughnessy at the end of the *Maltese Falcon* to explain why he's sending her where she belongs?)

II. The L.W.S. Hoax

The literary wise saying hoax is that specific Wise Sayings and Wise Comments in books and poems are applicable to life. If this were true then a person like me who hears Bob Dylan sing: "you'll find out when you've reached the top: you're on the bottom" could instantly stop worrying about the significance of his or her striving in Academia towards some sort of

(1) top or
(2) bottom-better-than-the-top or
(3) middle-that-is-somehow-better-than-either-top-or-bottom

(It occurs to me that my own Loyola University where I now work seems to me an Extremely, I mean Excruciatingly, Average American University. But I wonder what it is that forces me to think a thought like that, to relentlessly rank things in my mind???)

III. The A.A. Hoax

The Authorial Attitude Hoax is that it can be important in our own lives for us to identify with the supremely Superior Intelligence of the Author of a Great Book. If we think deeply about why she has created certain characters (non-characters) and invented a certain story (or non-story) to put them in and cause to turn out (or not turn out) a certain way and why she has written in a certain style (or lack of style) and what attitude she has towards her characters and her story—then we can learn how we ought to approach life that takes place outside books or, failing that, at least learn to understand at least something about how and why it is that real life in general and our own in particular defies all but ferociously false, stupidly simplistic (and self-deluding if they're self-congratulatory) understandings.

****

And what do Calvino and Ariosto have to say about these literary hoaxes?
Let me give some brief responses:

Response to U. C. H.

Ariosto and Calvino refuse to give us characters that are even remotely realistic. This should remind us that readers are woefully misguided if they try to change their life (or even end their life like some readers of Goethe's *Sorrows of Young Werther*) after reading about a character in a book.

Response to L.W.S.H.

Ariosto and Calvino undermine systematically their own wise comments or those of characters who are their obvious stand-ins or alter-egos. This means that one can always argue (and to prove the point even get into fist fights in rowdy bars) that all of the many wise comments and reflections on life and love in Ariosto and Calvino are in reality pseudo-wise comments that might well be utterly foolish.

Response to A.A.H.

Since both authors take care to call attention again and again and again to the unavoidable lies and contradictions one finds easily in literary works in general and in their own in particular, it is evident that Supreme Authorial Intelligences cannot guide us wherever it is we personally need to go.

(Granted, one must do something in life and come to some understanding of it—but the point or lack of point or point of lack is that on account of their very nature, books and their characters and wise sayings and oh-so-diabolically-intelligent authors can't help you figure out what to do.... And to lay it on thick one can even say a person has a better shot at figuring out things as well as they can be if she reads fewer serious literary works.)

What these responses amount to is the following irrefutable fact:

> READING THE BEST LITERATURE IS AS COMPLETE A WASTE OF TIME AS WATCHING T.V.

(And if Calvino speaks at the beginning of *(K)night II* of the battle between t.v. shows and serious literary texts like his for the passive attention of inert late twentieth-century consumers like you and me, he doesn't really give a truly unprejudiced observer any good reasons books like his must win out).

(I hope this wild negativity of demystification talk doesn't disturb you or bore you. But if you have trouble seeing through the falseness of this kind of negativity, then go buy some British punk albums and read the lyrics or information sheets they give out where they talk so nastily about what's wrong with everything—especially with teachers.)

(And come to think of it, there's no need to worry about this chapter at all—since it isn't particularly important anyway. It's just a set up for the next chapter where I write about the joke characters Ariosto and Calvino represent themselves with and the best false truths they manage to come up with to reflect maybe upon their own lives and careers.)

(And come to think of it, I'm glad this chapter isn't all that important: it's always best to postpone until some unspecified later date the Big Moment of Reckoning or Self-Reckoning when one asks a Big Question such as: Just what is it I'm doing in this profession? Should I try to get out of (or enter into or change drastically) my (a) relationship with X? Will the McDonald's invasion of the '90s totally ruin Italy?)

So, if you want, skip the rest of this chapter and go watch t.v. for the time segment you had allotted for reading it. (And if it happens to be Sunday I recommend the It's Gary Shandling's Show even though his self-deprecatory jokes are only funny once in a while—which of course is infinitely more than you can say about the equivalent in this book).

"Lies in Telling the Truth"—93

In letting the quotes from my authors flow, I could—if I felt like it—follow through on the three hoaxes I was using a minute ago and talk demystification precisely along those lies—I mean lines. But let's forget that stupid and arbitrary system entirely and change to the one in the following outline:

    I. Surprisingly Important Surface Material Considerations (SISMC)
        A. Books Are Made of Black Marks on White Pages
        B. Books Wind Up in a Totally Arbitrary Final Form

    II. High Frequency Demystificatory Themes (HFDT)
        A. Authors Are Nobodies
        B. Authors Are Flatterers of:
            1. The Powerful
            2. Their Prejudiced Readers
        C. Authors Are Not to Be Trusted Because :
            1. They Contradict Themselves
            2. They Lie Chronically

EXPLANATION OF OUTLINE:

I. A. The phony demystification game starts when one considers the material, physical, concrete existence of books of fiction. Literary books are consumer products in early as well as late capitalism and they always have and always will be (that kind of rhetoric in a chapter like this is thrown in as nonsense) consumer goods for people in certain social classes or income brackets that have received the costly educational training—that leads you to become imprisoned in a certain self image—and also have the leisure time to read and recognize certain books as products we need. It's certain, however, that these consumer products made out of black marks on white pages provide no real help in better understanding the strangely interrelated things like Power Sex Money Violence etc. that keep on baffling us as we try to understand how they affect our own lives.

I B: And if you think clearly about just how the book you are reading wound up in the form you are now reading it in, you realize how arbitrary that final form is: the author, driven by a mysterious logic of text construction (demanding order, variety, some kind of completeness etc.) has erased many words she might have used. And this must remind us (again) that whatever words wind up within the physical confines of a completed book can not help us understand our own infinitely less comprehensible life messes that change strangely as real time—so different from book and reading time—goes by).

(Even if we do think of ourselves in terms of stories with (even modestly) happy endings like "if I finish this book I'm writing and get good—or certain kinds of bad—reviews then I'll be the hero of the profession story" or "if I can make X agree to let me start explaining why I feel so lonely, then I'll be less unhappy at least for little while maybe" because it's unavoidable to think of ourselves in terms like that once we start thinking at all—our real—and impossible—task is to try to understand the limitations and inaccuracies of our self images and the stupidity of the only ways we know to go about seeking solutions to our problems in relation to our self images—in a way that books can't help us at all to do.)

II A: Authors are unimportant compared to political leaders whom they support directly or indirectly no matter what they write. (But their support is not essential to the political leaders whereas they could not write even in utter scorn of The Odious (Patriarchal, Capitalistic, Totalitarian Socialist etc.) System and the Useless Suffering It Inflicts unless an elitist order existed in which other people picked up their garbage and served them the wine of forgetfulness at Important Scholarly Gatherings.

II B.1. Authors are in fact always flatterers—either direct or indirect of those in power and no amount of latent irony, or overt cynicism or disdain towards the Stupid Powerful should induce us to forget how Literature supports the System.

II. B. 2. Authors are also forced to be shameless flatterers of their readers and self-censors so as not to really offend too much their readers' narrow tastes, expectations and class prejudices.

(Even authors who express open scorn for common-herd highbrow readers and even common-herd, horrifyingly un-insightful critics and professors—like me for example—and are sure they're

"Lies in Telling the Truth"—95

writing just for themselves as readers—EVEN THEY have inevitably acquired a censored taste—based too much on tradition—for what's possible and appropriate for their writings.)

III And indeed, (I must repeat because it's so important to me for some reason), authors and their critics don't deserve the importance they have never had and never will have because they contradict themselves and lie chronically. Some authors (like Bruce Springsteen) make every conceivable frenetic rhetorical effort to cover up their own partiality, internal contradictions and lies by attacking the partiality and lies of others. Springsteen—for example—teaches millions of too impressionable young Americans that you can learn more from a 3-minute song than from four years of high school or college.

But now we can let the quotes begin:

I A. (Note: The game in this first list of quotations and only in this first list is that I won't tell exactly where they're from—or even whether it's Calvino or Ariosto or part of a made-up connecting narration—although in general it will be obvious that Calvino is the most frequently quoted because he obsessively hammers into the anvil ideas expressed only once in a while by Ariosto.)

Italian version: "Una delle prime cose che devo dire è che un' opera di carta e d'inchiostro è solo un'opera di carta e inchiostro. E forse l'aver cominciato ... rievocando uno stato d'animo collettivo, una pazzia generale, mi fa dimenticare che sto parlando di un libro, roba scritta, righe di parole sulla pagina bianca. Anche se so che è assurdo parlare, per esempio, delle vie per cui l'anima o la società o l'inconscio si trasformano in una sfilza di righe nere su una pagina bianca.

In verità, ammetto che l'arte di scriver storie sta nel saper tirar fuori da quel nulla che si è capito della vita tutto il resto; ma finita la pagina si riprende la vita e ci s'accorge che quel che si sapeva è proprio un nulla. E dirò di più: La pagina ha il suo bene solo quando la volti e c'è la vita dietro che spinge e scompiglia tutti i fogli del libro.

Ma prima di incominciare questa storia parliamo per un momento delle persone che scrivono libri e il motivo per cui lo fanno. Possiamo dire che per sentieri d'inchiostro s'allontana al galoppo lo slancio guerriero della giovinezza, l'ansia esistenziale, l'energia dell'avventura spesi in una carneficina di cancellature e fogli appallottolati.

Non si può imprigionare l'esperienza in un libro e bisognerebbe tagliare tutti gli scritti e i libri e sino al cielo e fare alzare le minute schegge perché imitare la realtà e descrivere in un libro cose reali è ridicolo come si può vedere nei seguenti inizi tipici di romanzi che riscrivo in modo da dimostrarne l'assurdità:

1. Il romanzo comincia in una stazione ferroviaria, sbuffa una locomotiva, uno sfiatare di stantuffo copre l'apertura del capitolo, una nuvola di fumo nasconde parte del primo capo verso
2. Un odore di fritto aleggia ad apertura di pagina.
3. la prima sensazione che dovrebbe trasmettere questo libro è ciò che provo quando sento lo squillo di un telefono, dico dovrebbe perché dubito che le parole scritte possano darne un'idea anche parziale.
4. Queste pagine che sto scrivendo dovrebbero anch'esse comunicare una fredda luminosità da galleria di specchi, dove un numero limitato di figure si rifrange e si capovolge e si moltiplica.

Giacché un libro è solo fatto di parole si può benissimo anziché un libro scrivere degli elenchi di parole, in ordine alfabetico, una frana di parole isolate in cui si esprimono quella verità che ancora non conosco. E per concludere diciamo che tutti rigiriamo tra le mani un vecchio copertone vuoto mediante il quale vorremmo raggiungere il senso ultimo a cui le parole non giungono, ricordando allo stesso tempo che è impossibile concludere niente perché tutti sappiamo che sotto ogni parola c'è il nulla. E la parola veramente finale sulle conclusioni è che si finisce solo perché l'opera raggiunge una certa lunghezza e si è stanchi—non perché qualcosa è stato veramente concluso. E infatti, siccome tutti i fogli per questa parte sono pieni, voglio finirla e riposarmi.

(English: One of the first things I must say is that a work of paper and ink is decidedly only that. Any time I begin to try to bring to life in a book, say, the general spirit of Italy in the post World War II Renaissance, our country's general madness in those or other years, I quickly remember that I'm only writing a book. A book: written stuff, lines of words on a white page. And so it's absolutely absurd to speak, for example, of the ways in which one's soul or society or the subconscious are transformed into a string of black lines on a white page.

In truth, I readily admit that the art of writing stories is a question of knowing how to pull out from the Nothing-At-All that you've understood about life the All-The-Rest. And when you're done with the book and you begin life anew—you realize that what you knew is just that: Nothing At All. And I'll say even that the only good thing about pages in books is that when you turn them life is waiting in ambush to jump out and pull apart the pages of the book and fling them into an utterly confused pile.

And what kind of people *are* writers and why do they do it anyway? Well, we can say that along paths of ink, the writer takes off with a romping gallop, and his or her youthful combative energy, brooding anxiousness and drive for adventure are consumed in a massacre of erasures and crumpled sheets of paper. Or maybe in the ferocious pounding of the delete key on the word-processor keyboard.

The fact is—you really can't imprison experience in a book and we really ought to rip apart all writings and books and hurl their pieces skyward in minute fragments because it's ridiculous to open up a book and read about sounds and smells and visual images in works made out of paper and laser-printer ink. Let me rewrite some typical novel openings in a way that makes you think about just how strange it is to read about real world sensations in novels:

1. "My story begins in a train station where a locomotive is huffing and the steamy emissions of the piston are covering the chapter's opening and a cloud of smoke hides part of the first sentence."
2. "This story begins with a smell of fried foods hovering when you open up the book."
3. "This story transmits to you the sensation that I feel whenever I hear the sound of a telephone—I say "should transmit to you" because I doubt that written words could give even a limited idea of how much hearing a phone ring bothers me."
4. "This story that I'm writing is supposed to communicate to you the cold luminosity of a gallery of mirrors where a certain number of figures are refracted and reversed and multiplied."

98—HUMILITY'S DECEIT

You see, it's just absolutely hopeless to figure out what words to write down in a book. You might as well write lists of words in alphabetical order, an avalanche of isolated words to express truths we all need to know but just can't manage to figure out. The sad fact is that we all know there is some ultimate revelation we're seeking that words and books made out of words just can't lead us to. Because, really beneath every word lies nothingness and the last word at all on all conclusions is that you finish a book you're writing only because you've filled up a certain number of pages or because you've gotten tired—not because anything has been really said or concluded.)

I B. (Note: Ariosto uses weaving and music metaphors to make the same point that Calvino makes with his frequent self-driven moving machine metaphors)

Let's begin with Ariosto:

> far mi convien come fa il buono
> sonator sopra il suo instrumento arguto,
> che spesso muta corda, e varia suono,
> ricercando ora il grave, ora l'acuto.
>
> (As I write, I've got to make like the good
> musician playing on his sharp instrument
> who often changes strings and varies the sound
> strumming out now the low notes, now the high)

> Per una che biasmar cantando ardisco
> (che l'ordinata istoria così vuole),
> lodarne cento incontra m'offerisco,
> . . .
> ma tornando al lavor che vario ordisco . . .
>
> (For one woman that I dare to blame as I sing
> [just because my well-ordered story demands me to]
> I promise to praise a hundred others to make up for it
> . . .
> And now returning to the work that variously I warp [= weave on the loom])

"Lies in Telling the Truth"—99

ma prima che le corde rallentate
al canto disugual rendano il suono
fia meglio differirlo a un'altra volta
acciò men sia noioso a chi l'ascolta

(But before the slowed-up strings
make the sound in my song unbalanced
'twill be better to put it off to another time.
and make it less a bore to listeners of my rhyme.)

Calvino:

"In realtà il libro veniva fuori come per caso, m'ero messo a scrivere senza avere una trama precisa.... Era il racconto che—come sempre succede—imponeva soluzioni quasi obbligatorie."

(In truth the book kept coming out as if randomly, for I'd begun to write with no clear plot in mind . . . It was the tale that—the way it always goes—kept on forcing me into almost obligatory decisions)

"E' un processo che avviene automaticamente (cioé: guidare una macchina,) e se io stasera sono portato a rifletterci sopra è perché ora le possibilità esterne di distrazione diminuiscono quelle in me prendono il sopravvento . . . insomma devo fare uno sforzo particolare per concentrarmi sulla guida"

(Driving is a process that takes place automatically and if it happens that this evening I'm drawn to think this over it's because now that the outward chances that I'll get distracted lessen, inward possibilities of distraction increase . . . in short I have to make a special effort to concentrate on my driving)

Volare e il contrario del viaggio: attraversi una discontinuità dello spazio, sparisci nel vuoto, accetti di non essere in nessun luogo per una durata che e anch'essa una specie di vuoto nel tempo . . . ci vuole una buona dose d'incoscienza per affidarsi a congeni insicuri, approssimativamente guidati; (Ma stai riflettendo sul viaggio aereo o sulla lettura?)

(Flying is the opposite of a real voyage: you cross a discontinuity of space, you disappear into an emptiness, you agree to be no place at all for a period that is also a kind of emptiness in time . . . it takes a fair amount of foolhardiness to entrust yourself to an unsafe device, driven by imprecise instruments; [But reader, are you reflecting on your plane trip or on what happens when you read?])

II A. Ariosto

1. E vostri alti pensier cedino un poco
sì che tra lor i miei versi abbiano loco

(And let your lofty thoughts slide down a bit
to come down among my poor rhymes to sit)

II A. Calvino

1. "Lo scrittore è il più povero degli uomini"
(The writer is the poorest of men (SIC FEM)

2. "per questa donna io non sono altro che un'impersonale energia grafica, pronta a trasportare dall'inespresso alla scrittura un mondo immaginario che esiste indipendente da me"

(for this woman, I'm nothing more than an impersonal graphic energy, there only to pluck for the sake of the written page unexpressed things that come from an imaginary world that exists independently of me)

3. Il fatto è che lui più che affermare una sua verità vorrebbe fare delle domande. . . . Oppure vorrebbe che le domande le facessero gli altri a lui; . . . Comunque nessuno si sogna di chiedergli niente.

(Fact is that rather than affirm a particular truth of his own he prefers to ask some questions . . . or else he'd want questions from others to be asked of him . . . but not a soul has the least interest in asking him a fucking thing.)

II B. Ariosto Flatters His Boss Ippolito d'Este (Vice-President of Ferrara Motor Corporation)

1. "Quel ch'io vi debbo posso . . .
   pagare in parte . . .
   né che poco io vi dia da imputar sono,
   che quanto io posso dar, tutto vi dono."

   (What I owe you I can . . .
   pay only in part . . .
   nor for giving you so little, should you blame me
   because all I've got, I give, even if so very lamely)

2. Piacciavi, generosa Erculea prole,
   ornamento e splendor del secolo nostro,
   Ippolito, aggradir questo che vuole
   e darvi sol può l'umil servo vostro.

   (May it please you, generous Herculean offspring
   —ornament and splendor of our century—
   Ippolito, to accept this gift that is all
   your humble servant can offer you)

3. —fra tutti li signori illustri
   dal ciel sortiti a governar la terra,
   non vedi, o Febo, che 'l gran mondo lustri,
   più gloriosa stirpe o in pace o in guerra;

   (And among all the illustrious lords
   chosen by heaven to rule the earth,
   you see, o Phoebus, as you shine on the great world
   No family more glorious in peace or in war)

4. Ippolito, ch'a prose, a versi, a rime
   darà materia eterna in ogni idioma;

(Ippolito, who of praise in prose, verse, and rhyme
will be the eternal subject in all languages)

5. Poi cardinale appar, ma giovinetto,
sedere in Vaticano a consistoro,
e con facondia aprir l'alto intelletto
e far di sé stupir tutto quel coro.
—Qual fia dunque costui d'età perfetto?—
parean con maraviglia dir tra loro.
—Oh se di Pietro mai gli tocca il manto,
che fortunata età! che secol santo!—

(Then (I see a vision) of Ippolito, just a boy
seated in the Vatican at the Cardinal's council
where he abundantly displays his great intellect
and astonishes with his gifts the whole assemblage.
—What will then become of him at a mature age?—
they seemed with wonder to say to one another
—Oh if Peter's papal cloak should ever be won by him,
what a fortunate age! what a holy century!)

II B 1. Calvino Dissimulates His Flattery of the Powerful Through Grudging Acceptance of their Inevitable Mediocrity

1. "Palomar che dai poteri e dai contropoteri s'aspetta sempre il peggio, ha finito per convincersi che ciò che conta veramente è ciò che avviene nonostante loro."

(Palomar who from the powers and counterpowers always expects the absolute worst, has wound up convincing himself that what counts really is what happens *in spite* of them)

II B 2. Ariosto describes the ideal Renaissance reading public that he imagines waving to him from the shore as he pulls his ship into port at the end of his long poetic voyage:

"Oh di che belle e saggie donne veggio
oh di che cavallieri il lito adorno
Oh di ch'amici, a chi in eterno deggio
per la letizia c'han del mio ritorno."

(Oh what beautiful and wise women I see
and what fine gentleman over there adorning the shore!
o how eternally grateful I must be to my friends
for their joy at my safe return!)

II B 2. Calvino describes the ideal international sophisticated late twentieth-century reader and his (FEM SIC) advanced cynicism:

"Non che t'aspetti qualcosa di particolare da questo libro in particolare. Sei uno che per principio non s'aspetta più niente da niente. Ci sono tanti, più giovani di te o meno giovani, che vivono in attesa d'esperienze straordinarie; dai libri, dalle persone, dai viaggi, dagli avvenimenti, da quello che il domani tiene in serbo. Tu no . . ."

(It's not as if you expect anything in particular out of this book. You're one who as a rule doesn't expect anything out of anything. There are so many, younger than you or even less young, that live in expectation of extraordinary experiences; from books, from people, from trips, from events, from whatever tomorrow holds in store. You're not that kind of fool . . .)

III A. Ariosto
1. The narrator leads us to believe that Sacripante is a fool to believe Angelica's story that she is a virgin:

Quel che l'uom vede, Amor gli fa invisibile,
e l'invisibil gli fa vedere Amore.
Questo creduto fu; che 'l misero suole
dar facile credenza a quel che vuole.

(What a man sees, Love makes invisible to him
and the invisible love makes him see
This was believed; because a poor wretch usually
can't help believing what he needs to be sure of)

(I know I'm not supposed to comment here. But I can't help it. Because this quote happens to remind me so much of the *Boxer* that I used to self-indulgently identify with so much a long long time

ago. That song tells us that "a man (fem sic! sic! sic!) hears what he wants to hear and disregards the rest.")
But we learn that she was in fact telling the truth:

> Angelica a Medor la prima rosa
> coglier lasciò, non ancor tocca inante:
> né persona fu mai sì avventurosa,
> ch'in quel giardin potesse por le piante.

> (Angelica let Medor her very first rose
> pluck off the stem, never touched before:
> nor had anyone been ever so lucky
> that in that garden could get in at all)

2. Ariosto tells us that men who practice any sort of violence against women violate all laws of God and nature:

> parmi non sol gran mal, ma che l'uom faccia
> contra natura e sia di Dio ribello,
> che s'induce a percuotere la faccia
> di bella donna, o romperle un capello;

> (Seems to me not only a great ill, but an act
> against nature and a rebellion against God,
> anytime a man brings himself to strike the face
> of a beautiful woman or harm even a single hair)

But he sympathizes entirely with Orlando when he decides to murder Angelica for not giving him what all men think they automatically deserve from women they fall in love in. And he gets so carried away in his rancor against all the women in the world that he condones all the psychological and physical violence against them that men are "justly" driven to. Ariosto is sorry that Orlando fails to get his murderous hands on Angelica's evil neck and wishes that his hero could grab and kill not only her but all women on earth:

> "Né questa sola, ma fosser pur state
> in man d'Orlando quante oggi ne sono;
> ch'ad ogni modo tutte sono ingrate,
> né si trova tra loro oncia di buono.

"Lies in Telling the Truth"—105

(If only—not only this one alone—but all the other ones had wound up in Orlando's hands: yeah! every last woman! Because they're *all* ingrates in just the same way: You can't find an ounce of good in any woman alive today.)

III. A. Calvino: A writer alter-ego of Calvino, Silas Flannery tells us that he writes only in the hope of living to write to contradict himself in the future:

"Se . . . penso che sto scrivendo un'intera biblioteca, mi sento improvvisamente alleggerito: so che qualsiasi cosa io scriva sarà integrata, contradetta, bilanciata, amplificata, sepolta dalle centinaia di volumi che mi restano da scrivere."

("If . . . I think that I'm writing a whole library, I feel less encumbered all of a sudden: I know that whatever I happen to write will be integrated contradicted, balanced, expanded upon and buried by the hundreds of volumes that remain for me to write.")

III B 1. Ariosto
1. After we have seen that Alcina is not the beautiful woman described earlier but an old toothless hag, Ariosto exclaims with phony anguish:

Oh quante incantatrici, oh quanti
incantator tra noi, che non si sanno!

(Oh how many enchantresses, o how many male enchanters live among us, without our knowing them for what they are)

But later on in the poem, we learn that male poets fall under that category of male enchanters and are every bit as treacherous as perfidious female enchantresses. For they too, it turns out, always try to convince readers that false things are true:

"Omero Agamennòn vittorioso
e fe' i Troian parer vili et inerti;
e che Penelopea fida al suo sposo

> dai Prochi mille oltraggi avea sofferti.
> E se tu vuoi che 'l ver non ti sia ascoso,
> tutta al contrario l'istoria converti:
> che i Greci rotti, e che Troia vittrice,
> e che Penelopea fu meretrice."
>
> (Homer told us Agamemon was heroic victor
> and made out the Trojans to be cowards and wimps
> and told us Penelope was true to her groom
> and forced to suffer a thousand Terrible Outrages.
> But if you want the truth to be no longer hidden
> turn contrariwise his whole fake story:
> because the Greeks were routed and *Troy* the victory bore
> and Penelope actually was a just slimy little whore.

III B. Calvino

Calvino tells us that no matter how hard authors try to tell the truth the whole truth and nothing but the truth—an open-minded, sharply scrutinizing reader will never fail to find absolutely indubitable falseness in any author or teacher's most deeply prized profound truths:

> le falsità senza attenuanti nelle parole che si pretendono più veritiere."
>
> (falseness that simply can't be explained away in whatever words you are claiming to be as true as you can possible make them)

A FINAL NOTE TO AN UNIMPORTANT CHAPTER:
The Two Kinds of Wise Literary Truths Revisited
And Why Not To Believe Them

Ariosto's Positive Wisdom

The *Furioso* is full of wise sayings and exhortations to good conduct. Take the following celebration of the importance of keeping one's faith (one of a large number on that particularly chivalric knightly virtue) for example:

> La fede unqua non debbe esser corrotta,
> o data a un solo, o data insieme a mille;
> e così in una selva, in una grotta,
> lontan da le cittadi e da le ville,
> e come dinanzi a tribunali, in frotta
> di testimon, di scritti e di postille,
> senza giurare o segno altro più espresso,
> basti una volta che s'abbia promesso
>
> (A promise must never ever be broken
> whether given to one person alone or given before a
> [thousand
> and the same thing holds in a wood or in a cave
> far from our cities and country villages
> as holds in our courtrooms, with all the crowds
> of witnesses, the written reports and the notes,
> where with no sworn statements nor no special sign
> it should be enough to just promise once and say "I'll do it,
> [fine!")

It's also clear enough that Ariosto realizes that this critique of a stupid litigation-obsessed society overflowing with idiotic complicated forms and contracts and Fulbright NEH etc. fellowship applications (for which just a simple phoned in promise to do diligent fine work should be more than enough since the only fair way to award those things is by lottery) is far too simplistic.

(If you thought you were going to escape an invective against Academic Fellowship Competitions—no such luck. I mean, Jesus Christ! the fact is you always get these committees of Boring Senior Scholars that decide fellowship competitions in favor of only people recommended by their close friends and cronies. The more I think about it, the more I can't believe I didn't quit Academia years ago.)

And why am I saying Ariosto's exhortations to keep the faith are too simplistic? Well, in this case, the lesson here is the moral derived from some obviously ridiculous business in Canto 19 where earnest Zerbino's word-of-mouth promise requires him to be the defender of the ludicrous and perfidious hag Gabrina. And while we're on the subject of laughing at ugly women, to return (oh no not again! . . .) to the Big Problem of Women, everytime Ariosto "praises" women and says he's their sincerely feminist friend, he always does so right after or right before an action sequence in which women are being implicitly sneered at with the usual men's club cynicism about how ridiculous women basically are (nowadays countered of course by no lack of women's club cynicism about how ridiculous prisoner-of-the penis men are)

Do you remember the passage I quoted two chapters ago that starts:

> Le donne son venute in eccellenza
> di ciascun'arte ove hanno posto cura . . .
>
> (Women have achieved excellence
> in every art in which they've placed their care)

Well, what I didn't mention there was that this feminist manifesto is in the middle of the episode in Ariosto in which we're introduced to a race of vengeful, murderous females (the ones you might remember I told you Astolpho sends fleeing with his horrible horn) who, among other outrageous oppressions decapitate men who can't satisfy ten women—one after the other—in bed. And I'm pretty sure they aren't allowed to sneak in any artificial sex-shop objects (of a sort I simply can't imagine in actual use, can you?):

> Prima ne fur decapitati molti
> che riusciro al paragon mal forti . . .
>
> (First many of them were decapitated
> who turned out to be not strong enough for that tough test)

in which all the old male paranoia about how hard it is to satisfy women comes out. And of course the traditional idea that it is impossible to please women no matter what you do is still just as firmly in place today in some stunning lyrics from the Prince song "Listen to the Doves' Cry." I mean where he sings darkly "Maybe I'm just like my mother . . . she's never satisfied."

(Truth is we men all realize we may not be as different from women as we've always hoped. Personally an academic like me sick of his own and everybody else's work can identify particularly with Prince's and his mother's desperation.)

Negative Truths Undone

But if Ariosto's game is letting us see the patent falsity of any simple cheerful positive wisdom of the kind that's so big on American TV: "Say yes to a whole lot more"; "Be all you can be," Calvino's game is an opposite that—of course—amounts to exactly the same thing as Ariosto's.

Calvino reveals the patent falseness inherent in all Dark, Disquieting, Terrible and Horrible Negative Truths about Existence, precisely the kind that certain mirthless academics love so much to gravely point out as if it were reality and not they themselves that were so sour because their jobs are so pointless and disappointing.

As it happens the Three Major Negative Truths that Calvino makes fun of are perhaps

(1) All choices are anguishingly arbitrary
(2) All relationships are fatally undermined by an unavoidable mutual incomprehension
(3) All exchanges of ideas between the generations, between the young and the old, between parents and children, teachers and students are fruitless

1. We Ain't Got No Choice

"La storia dell'indeciso": "Ogni volta che sta per decidere quale delle due gli conviene come sposa, si convince che può benissimo rinunciare all'altra, e così si rassegna a perdere questa ogni volta che s'accorge di preferire quella. L'unico punto fermo in questo va e vieni di pensieri è che può fare a meno sia dell'una che dell'altra, perché ogni scelta ha un rovescio cioè una rinuncia, e così non c'è differenza tra l'atto di scegliere e l'atto di rinunciare."

("Every time he's on the verge of deciding which of the two would just the right bride for him (situational FEM SIC!), he tells himself he can very well give up the other, and so he accepts having to lose the latter every time he realizes he prefers the former. The only stable point in this ebb and flow of thought is that he can do without either one, for every choice has its opposite, that is to say a refusal, and so there is no difference between the act of choosing and the act of refusing")

2. Only Imbeciles Expect Anything Out of Marriages or Friendships

Another phony negative truth is that all relationships are doomed to bleak failure. The story "Priscilla" in *Ti con zero* is a joke biology lesson that teaches us science illiterates the limited amount of info overrated (and overindulged by governmental funding agencies) scientists have figured out so far about how the characteristics of the individual are determined by the mixing of genes when her mother's and father's cells meet at the moment of conception. In the biology lesson story, Calvino throws in casually his usual Devastating Eternal Negative Truths (hereafter: DENTS) about the necessary failure of all relationships.

He starts and finishes a long paragraph describing what exactly happens in the meeting in the fallopian tube of a sperm and egg cell:

> Beginning: "La separazione, l'impossibilità d'incontrarsi è già in noi da principio. Siamo nati non da una fusione ma da una giustappposizione di corpi diversi . . .
>
> (Separation, the impossibility of meeting one another is already in us from the start. We're born not from a fusion but from a mere juxtaposition of two different bodies . . .)
>
> End: Intanto il doppio nucleo ha dato inizio alla sequela delle sue duplicazioni, stampando i messagggi abbinati

del padre e della madre in ognuna delle cellule figlie, perpetuando non tanto l'unione quanto la distanza incolmabile che separa in ogni coppia i due compagni, il fallimento, il vuoto che rimane in mezzo alla coppia più riuscita."

(Meanwhile the double nucleus has begun the sequence of its duplications, printing the combined messages from father and mother in each and every one of the daughter cells, perpetuating not so much the union as the unbridgeable distance that separates the two partners in every couple, the failure, the emptiness that's always there even in the most successful couple.)

3. What A Drag It Is Getting Old And Having to Talk to Young People

Speaking of the vastly overemphasized-in-literature problem of Assured Mutual Incomprehension Between Any Two Human Beings (AMIBAT-HB virus), another thing that obsessively interests Calvino is how impossibile it is for the old and young to understand one another even slightly. In *Castle of Destinies*, Calvino derives a bleak lesson about the futility of parent-child relationships from Shakespeare's *King Lear*. He says:

Con le figlie, qualsiasi cosa faccia un padre, sbaglia: autoritari o permissivi che siano, ai genitori nessuno dirà mai grazie: le generazioni si guardano torve, si parlano solo per non capirsi, per darsi a vicenda la colpa di crescere infelici e di morire delusi.

(With a daughter, whatever a father does is all wrong: whether authoritarian or permissive, parents will never receive any thanks: The generations stare angrily at each other, they speak only to misunderstand each other, to attack each other for having to grow up miserable and die disappointed.")

But isn't it obvious that Calvino's glib negative clichés about the impossibility of everything are just as shallow as Ariosto's conventional moralizing wisdom?

So Ariosto's implicit critique of positive edifying remarks about how nice the world would be if people could learn to be simple and good and true corresponds precisely to Calvino's critique of negative anti-edifying remarks about how it is impossible to get anything truly important in life even ever so slightly right.

What happens (strangely) with Calvino is that we are pushed paradoxically to strain somehow toward Impossible Optimism about Life that irrepressibly stirs in our souls (or genital areas or wherever). Because we see in Calvino that serious literature's tendency toward negative truths is just as suspect as the tendency in self-help books like *Women Men Love, Women Men Leave* towards positive truths.

(I would imagine from the title of that book that my own absurd prejudices won't allow me to read that women who read the book are supposed to be able learn to be the type that keeps their men forever and have the most wonderful mature loving relationships that one can possibly have in this life.

But, as I was saying, if the promise of Simple Truths to Help Us Get Our Lives Back on Track makes me and maybe—or maybe not—you—sneer, so too should the negative ones of literary texts.

So we reach a final impasse: Any truth about life whether of the positively encouraging sort "it could be better if only we tried a little harder to make it a little better" or of the negatively unencouraging sort "things are this bad because that's just the way it's gotta be and God knows we're lucky it's not a whole lot worse and Hitler isn't even more overtly ruling everywhere" can be placed in a fictional or critical text not to decide anything about their truth value but only to be undermined, shown to be limited, joked about, thrown right out the window.

But let me end this chapter by phonily acknowledging my own ridiculousness in trying to make claims about the nature of the nontruth of thoroughly demystified literature in such an assertive way: as if my claims were not themselves misleading lies.

So if you somehow think what I'm getting at in this chapter is that we need to strike a balance between positivity and trying to make ourselves and the world better than it is and negativity and trying to resign ourselves to the bleakness of life on this perverted planet and somehow learn to inhabit a middle ground from which you see the importance of both attitudes and the importance of shifting attitudes as much as possible (the natural flow of consciousness between exhilaration and despair from minute to minute or hour to hour—the kind of mood shifts you become especially aware of when you're in the grip of an obsessive erotic passion). YOU COULDN'T BE MORE WRONG.

CHAPTER FIVE

CAN CALVINO'S HUMILITY REALLY NOT BE PROUD?

Now that I've reached this last and final chapter of *Ariosto's Parrot(s)* (or did I end up deciding on some other title?) I should mimic for the one or two of you still on deck my authors' remarks about their storm-battered ships sailing into tranquil port at wearying journey's conclusion. Well, sorry one more time to disappoint you.

(Having just made that phony little remark about the one or two readers still remaining, I feel the need to be a little more honest—since, after all, this is my last chance at any kind of truth. Well—truth is—I don't care at all if there are no readers at all left. People like me write more to communicate in weird ways with themselves than to communicate with others. And it's not as if I really care whether or not you like or don't like my stupid thought patterns. Because it's not as if you'd expect me to think just the way you do, would you?)

This chapter we're talking nude truth, no question about it. We've seen how Ariosto and Calvino did long softcore body-part inventories on Olimpia and Bradamante. Now we're going to look at how they strip themselves just as naked. How they hold up to our voyeuristic gaze the unattractive anatomy of their male minds. (Or is it female minds, because so shifting and unstable?)

Yes, yes. I know I've already (unless I somehow forgot) said that Ariosto and Calvino are two of the most un-autobiographical authors that have ever existed on the senseless earth or the lunatic moon. Neither ever lets us know anything real about his life and loves. Both hide timidly behind literary games and conventions as if they were scared professors taking refuge in academic games and conventions. And, Calvino on occasion even harshly derides authors who wear their hearts on their sleeve—as if to say such a charge could never be levelled at him.

(I've done my best to avoid finding out anything about what Calvino was like in real life—but on a recent pointless trip to

"Can Calvino's Humility Really Not Be Proud?"—115

Rome—I was staring one afternoon at the Calvino nameplate on the apartment building near the Pantheon in which he lived until his death in 1985 and a grinning stranger came up to me, looked me in the eyes and said in accented English: "You know *Palomar* was the book he really put all of himself into. I could tell the time he called me up and asked me in a certain way what I thought of it. And you know, he wasn't at all envious of other Italian writers. You just kind of knew that he knew he was the best.")

Yes, in this chapter I am interested in celebrity secrets—but of a slightly different kind than normal. I am interested in my authors' secret selves only as they reveal them in their books. But only because I want to think a little about what their secret selves might have to do with mine.

I want to go a lot deeper into myself than I've gone so far in this book. So if now you think of me as merely a below average professor in his mid-thirties under obligation to waste readers' time in (more or less) Scholarly Works of importance only to the Various Deans of Loyola University of Chicago (those overpaid smooth-talkers at various bureaucratic levels with Wildly Bold Dreams of their own University becoming The Harvard of the Next Millennium), in this chapter I'll show you unsuspected levels of my human depth.

(Here at Loyola these days the Deans tell us professors that we can become the premier Catholic Research Institution in the Universe if we'd all spend 20 hours per weekend at our word processors for the next ten years. Come on! As if St. Augustine had never existed to talk in his phony *Confessions* about how little that kind of thinking has to do with Catholicism (see page 30 or somewhere around there in the Penguin edition) and how much it would displease Christ—who in my opinion if He (fem sic) were around would enjoy preaching against the arrogance of most of the Important Humanity Scholars around here. Why doesn't someone tell my bosses to find some other game-show category under which to dream unChristianly about Loyola University of Chicago's promising future? Why don't they say "let's make Loyola the best university among those whose basketball team has won one and only one NCAA title"?)

All right, all right, all right. I'll stop being so naive. And stop digressing. As if I were just idly filling up page after page and had nothing at all to say.

Well then, without further ado, it is obvious enough to see that Ariosto is:

1. Himself, the smooth-talking, modest regular guy who talks about his own problems and about Ferrari's, the one we imagine to be a nice guy always basically in control.

2. Orlando the passionate masochist who desires someone he knows he can't have on purpose—because what he really desires is the unequaled sweet intensity of self-pity in the rejection experience.

And it is a little less obvious but quite plausible to see him also in:

3. Rodomonte
4. Bradamante

I'll say just why I think so in just a minute.

But first we have to tackle—or better: make our fast break towards—scoring a quick solution to the more difficult problem of figuring out which of the many stand-ins for Calvino ought to be the gang of four I can choose to match Ariosto's.

To start with, we need another chart. Here it is and it's not at all complete:

THE "CALVINO HIMSELF" CHARACTERS IN CALVINO'S BOOKS

Book: Calvino Character(s)

Spider: Pin, Dritto
Count Badgood: Both Medardos, boy
Treeboy: Cosimo, brother narrator
A Thin Knight: Rambaldo, Bradamante
Smoggy: Bureaucrat intellectual
(Not the Sony) Watchman: The (partying) watchman
Marcovaldo: Marcovaldo
Comicon: qwfwg the nerd
Tease: qwfwg and Farias/Dumas
Cross Author's Destinies: Orlando, Me, Bradamante, Faust, Devil
(Rodomonte), waverer, Hamlet, Macbeth, Lear

"Can Calvino's Humility Really Not Be Proud?"—117

Cityminds: I don't understand this work at all but I do like it since it contains some great passages. (Read through it some day if you haven't yet.)
Winter (K)night Ta(i)les: All ten "me-s,"Silas, Hermes, Manreader, Girlie reader (Ludmilla), police-censor, all the professor-types in the library and really just about everybody

(No) Pals For Me: Palomar, guide of the school boys in the Aztec temple, clumsy male turtle, desolate Albino gorilla

Among these characters, we find that the following four are based photocopicly on the Ariosto four:

1. Smogcloud main character
2. Palomar
3. Pin
4. Ludmilla

So let's get to work.

PART ONE
Ariosto Himself and Mr. Smogcloud

This is the starting point for talking about what Ariosto and Calvino are really like as human beings. No of course not. No one is "really like" anything. There are only points of view: your own about yourself and those of others who, incidentally, like me, care infinitely more about themselves than about you.

Ariosto presents himself in stanzas 3 and 4 of his very first canto as a very graciously humble courtier. He immediately, (as you saw on page 101) begins to flatter Cardinal Ippolito d'Este, coruler of the kingdom of Ferrara (the way all of us parasite academics do any time we talk to people who have the power to give us raises). Literature, he reminds Ippolito, is lowly business and serves only as occasional distraction from the serious business of life in the real world: which in Ippolito's typical case is: making money and war in the world and making love at home (I think) under steamy Titian bedroom imitation-playboy-pinup paintings— which I guess I envy him for, stupidly.

But let's go right to Calvino's Mr. Smogcloud to find out more about why Ariosto is so into phony self-deprecation.

(I might have chosen the guy in the "Watchman Story" as the best equivalent of the Ariosto himself character. He is in fact a close second but he loses out because his relationship with the woman is too messed-up in a normal way. Whereas Smogcloud's weird relationship with the chic lady is dazzlingly strange).

Mr. Smogcloud has taken a job in a city like Turin as managing editor of a publication called *Purification* but he is adamant in expressing his utter indifference to this job and all jobs, especially those with missions. A job for Mr. Smogcloud is something one only has to pretend to take seriously: "I had accepted the job just as a last resort, and now I had to act as if I had never thought of anything else in my whole life."

And in the title of the publication Smogcloud works for: "Purification,"Calvino is thinking especially about writers and teachers . Since isn't "important" fiction-writing and "the best" teaching about works of fiction somehow supposed to help purify students' and other professors' smogclouded minds and lay the groundwork for cleaning up our morally polluted society maybe starting next generation?

But Calvino uses the title "Purification" only to take such illusions away from us and bluntly tells us (and himself) that as a writer-teacher, he has to learn to resign himself to being an insignificant bureaucrat in modern technological society, someone whose job is no more meaningful than the next gal's.

("It's my work', he'd say, I do it for pay and when it's over I'd just as soon be on my way" is a line Bob Dylan seems to identify with quite a bit when he imagines Rubin "Hurricane" Carter expressing that thought in one of those famous songs in which Dylan makes big money by devising very interesting rhymes ("put his ass in the stir" rhymed brilliantly with "pin this triple murder") on the trite "Don't it make you feel ashamed/to live in a land/where justice is a game???") theme. As if people in power who dispense "justice" weren't just as evil everywhere in whatever system.)

But the question now is: if an uncompromising humility is so important to Ariosto and Calvino's—how then do other aspects of their secret selves relate to their humility?

Glad you asked me. Let me start with Bradamante and Ludmilla.

PART TWO

Bradamante and Ludmilla

(By now I hope you've forgotten what I said about these two in Chapter Two because what I say here has nothing at all to do with that discussion.)

True Humility should lead one straight to lucid common-sense acceptance of life and its overwhelming limitations. Many women, we are told (too often for some, not often enough for others, these days), typically have a limited, low-expectations life forced on them either directly by society or indirectly by society's internalized voice within them—assuming biology (hormones and stuff?) has nothing to do with it. Surprisingly enough, the self-constraints that some women come to place on themselves might give everyone just the right idea for how to live. (Or rather I mean somehow the least stupid idea among all unacceptable alternatives.)

Both Bradamante and Ludmilla are modern (Renaissance modern or late 20th Century modern, take your pick) but at-heart traditional women who have the very same qualities I admire and envy in my very very favorite young women students at Loyola. Self-assured but humble at the same time, both these young women are curious, eagerly intelligent, straightforward, and passionate in an appropriately reserved way. In addition, they are faithful to one man at a time or to an image of an ideal man and more interested in supporting their friends and family and not disconcerting anyone's expectations than in satisfying their own egos. Above all, they are instinctively cheerful in accepting the limitations that life imposes on us all.

Here are examples of all these positive traits in Bradamante (=B) and Ludmilla (=L) as described by our authors:

> Healthy curiosity: Questo disir, ch'a tutti sta nel core,
> de' fatti altrui sempre cercar novella,
> fece a quel cavallier del suo dolore
> la cagione domandar da la donzella
>
> (This desire, that is found in everyone's heart
> of finding out what's going on in other people's lives
> made the damsel [B] ask that knight
> about the reason for his grief)

Eager intelligence: "Il guaio è che lei di romanzi ne ha letti molti di più di te, specialmente stranieri, e ha una memoria minuziosa, allude a degli episodi precisi, ti domanda: "e ricorda cosa dice la zia di Henry quando..."

("The only trouble is that she's [L's] read a lot more novels than you, especially foreign ones, and she has a memory for details, and makes references to specific episodes asking you things like "and do you remember what Henry's aunt says when...")

Straightforwardness: "Credi che a un certo punto potresti avere diritto [di fare una scenata di gelosia]? Se è così è meglio non cominciare neppure."

("Do you think that sometime you *could* have the right to make a jealous scene? If that's the way it is, we're better off not even starting.")

Passionate Nature: Baciò la carta diece volte e diece,
avendo a chi la scrisse il cor diritto.
Le lacrime vietàr, che su vi sparse,
che con sospiri ardenti ella non l'arse.

(She (B) kissed the letter ten times and ten times more having her heart set on the one who wrote it.
Her tears that she shed on it stopped
her burning sighs from burning the letter all up.)

Self-Restraint (unlike men like Orlando and Silas Flannery who allow mindless male lust to make them forget all restraints):

"E' tutto un equivoco, Mister Flannery—dice Ludmilla, e si ferma, frapponendo tra noi la mole del dizionario universale Webster—io potrei benissimo far l'amore con lei; lei è un signore gentile e d'aspetto gradevole. Ma questo non avrebbe nessuna rilevanza nel problema che stavamo discutendo... Non avrebbe niente a che fare con l'autore Silas Flannery di cui leggo i romanzi."

(It's a complete misunderstanding, Mr. Flannery—Ludmilla says, and she stops, placing between us the mass of Webster's Universal Dictionary—I could very well make love with you; you're a nice man and have a pleasant appearance. But this would have no relevance to the problem that we were discussing . . . It would have nothing to do with the author Silas Flannery whose novels I read.)

Fidelity: "Ma vo' prima morir, che mai sia vero
ch'io pigli altro marito che Ruggiero"

("But I want first to die than it ever to be true
that I accept another man, Ruggiero, as husband than you"

Domani Lettore e Lettrice, se sarete insieme, se vi coricherete nello stesso letto come una coppia assestata, ognuno accenderà la lampada . . . e sprofonderà nel suo libro; . . . Ma non ironizzate su questa prospettiva di armonia coniugale: quale immagine di coppia più fortunata sapreste contrapporle?

(Tomorrow Reader and Reader, if you're together, if you're getting ready to go to sleep in the same bed as a settled couple, each of you will turn on the reading lamp and will plunge into his or her book . . . But don't be sarcastic about this kind of marital harmony: what image of a luckier couple could you come up with to beat this one?)

Self-sacrificing: Sta Bradamante tacita, né al detto
de la madre s'arrisca a contradire;
che l'ha in tal riverenzia e in tal rispetto,
che non potria pensar non l'ubbidire.

(Bradamante is silent, nor the words
of her mother does she dare contradict
because she holds her in such reverence and such esteem
that of not obeying Mom she cannot even dream)

Sensitivity to Others (Bradamante and Ludmilla are the rare type of person we truly look forward to running into on the street. In a world where more and more people are career-driven robots chasing stupid cliched dreams of professional and personal fulfillment—people who can talk only about themselves and their gifted children and their stupid job and their stupid emotional problems and how unfair life is to them—, Bradamante and Ludmilla are the kind of people who remember how to act. They always say just the right kind of friendly, reassuring, traditional thing and remember how to make people they talk to feel all right for at least a little while): —Oh ma sei proprio tu! Ogni volta che passo sulla Prospettiva t'incontro! Non mi dirai che passi le giornate a passeggio! Senti, conosco un caffé qui all'angolo, pieno di specchi, con un'orchestra che suona dei valzer: m'inviti?

(Oh but it really is you! Every time I take a walk on the Prospect I meet you! Now don't tell me you spend your days strolling around? Say, I know a café here at the corner, full of mirrors with an orchestra that plays waltzes: will you take me there?)

(It is actually a character named Franziska that says this but it might as well be Ludmilla—since from Chapter Six on of *If a (K)night*, we learn to take every female character as either Ludmilla or Lotaria)

PART THREE

Pin and Rodomonte: The Rage of Frustration

But it isn't always so easy to accept limitations. Sometimes, like adolescents, we fantasize revenge against everything that imprisons us.
So it happens that Rodomonte and Pin, two of our authors' most memorable characters have something of their writers and of me and you in them.
In this section let's play a little game of beginnings and endings. O. K.?
At the very end of *Orlando Furioso*, Rodomonte dies with a curse:

"Can Calvino's Humility Really Not Be Proud?"—123

> Bestemmiando fugì l'alma sdegnosa
> Che fu sì altiera al mondo e sì orgogliosa
>
> (Cussing blasphemies that disdaining soul fled to Hell
> A soul that was so haughty in this world and so very proud)

And at the very beginning of Calvino's Developing Lifelong Poem, on the first page of *Spiderboy*, Calvino starts firing insults. Pin's central insult in an initial series of three is of course a put down of a wanton woman:

> ... Ciao Carolina, meno male quella volta. Sì, quella volta meno male tuo marito che non ha guardato sotto il letto.
>
> (Hi Carolina, got pretty fucking lucky that time, huh. Yeah, fuckin' lucky that time your husband didn't look under the bed)

Rodomonte and Pin are constantly at odds with society, always sadly left out. Pin is a child puzzled by the strange world of adults and their games involving weapons and (of course) women. Just what weapons and women are for and how in hell one is supposed to use the one or the other mystifies him thoroughly:

> E' triste essere come lui, un bambino nel mondo dei grandi, sempre un bambino, trattato dai grandi come qualcosa di divertente e di noioso; e non potere usare quelle loro cose misteriose ed eccitanti, armi e donne, non potere far mai parte dei loro giochi.
>
> (It's sad to be like him, a kid in a world of grownups, always a kid, treated by grownups like something fun and something boring; and to not be able to use those mysterious and exciting things of theirs—arms and women, not to be able to take part in their games)

And in Ariosto's "women and weapons" poem: (Le donne, i cavalier, le armi gli amori ... io canto: [Women, Knights, Arms, Loves, ... I sing]) Rodomonte's brutal rejection at the hands of Doralice leads this thoroughly adolescent man to insult all women. Here is the culminating stanza of a four and a half stanza assault in which lines five through seven contain *eleven* separate venomous putdowns of all women:

> Non siate però tumide e fastose,
> donne, per dir che l'uom sia vostro figlio;
> che de le spine ancor nascon le rose,
> d'una fetida erba nasce il giglio:
> importune, superbe, dispettose,
> prive d'amor, di fede e di consiglio,
> temerarie, crudeli, inique, ingrate,
> per pestilenzia eterna al mondo nate.—
>
> (Don't be, on that account, swelled up and proud,
> women, 'cause you can say that man is your son;
> you know: from thorns are born roses
> and from stinking grass is born the lily:
> arrogant, haughty, disrespectful
> loveless, faithless, brainless:
> brazen, cruel, wicked, ungrateful
> an eternal pestilence born into the world.)

Unable to relate to women in particular and everyone in general, completely excluded from society, both Pin and Rodomonte have mountains of frustration that gnaw at them. Each expresses his anguish as often as possible either in wantonly violent words (Pin) or in wantonly violent action (Rodomonte):

Pin

> "Alé—fa Pin, con le labbra che gli tremano, pallido. Sa che non può cantare. Vorrebbe piangere, invece scoppia in uno strillo in "i" che schioda i timpani e finisce in uno scatenio di improperi: —Bastardi, figli di quella cagna impestata di vostra madre vacca sporca lurida puttana!—
>
> (All right! goes Pin, with his lips trembling, all pale. He knows he can't sing. He'd prefer to cry, but he bursts out in a squealy "ee" sound that busts your eardrums and winds up in a rapid-fire shooting of insults: —Bastards, sons of that filthy bitch of a mother of yours—fucking cow slimeball whore—)

> Rodomonte
>
> ... che qualunche s'adagia, il re d'Algiere,
> Rodomonte crudele, uccide o fere,
>
> sol Rodomonte sprezza di venire
> se non dove la via meno è sicura.
> Dove nel caso disperato e rio
> gli altri fan voti, egli bestemmia Dio.
>
> (... whoever is slow to retreat, the king of Algiers
> Cruel Rodomonte murders or wounds
>
> only Rodomonte will come in
> where the road is least secure.
> Whereas others in desperate, horrible situations
> make oaths to God, he curses Him.)

The adolescent spirit in Ariosto and Calvino (who remind us often that they find it impossible to grow up properly and continue to suggest that writer-teacher-serious readers are essentially maladjusted children in an adult world of people smart enough to avoid taking reading seriously) is curious in authors of such immense literary polish and sophistication. Perhaps they mean to apologize for their sophistication by identifying with adolescent characters.

PART FOUR

Orlando and Palomar

This is where we really wanted to get to. The most important character for both authors. At least as my story goes.

I've already talked enough about Ariosto's Orlando. The mad character, the one out of phase, the one who can't retain his common sense and can't express adolescent frustrations in the normal channels of speaking and acting that we all develop.

(Professors, for example, release their frustrations by insulting students and giving them poor grades and by insulting rivals and giving them poor reviews—because neither class of imbecile shows anywhere near proper respect for our Insights and Wisdom.)

But unlike two chapters ago, here I'm going to associate Ariosto's Orlando with Palomar, who in the story I'm making up becomes the character who best explains Everything.

But of course the structure of this arbitrary book demands that I give equal time to Ariosto in this section. But how can I fit him in?

Well, how about if we relate the madness business to the general problem we all have of relating properly to other human beings. Let's consider for a moment the system of all the moralizing intros to all of Ariosto's 46 cantos (like that "be all you can be! ladies" feminist pitch and the one about the importance of keeping our promises I quoted for you last chapter).

What I find to be (or can invent as) the plan behind Ariosto's introductions is the following:

1. In the early canto intros, Ariosto presents some disturbing observations about how impossible it is to relate to others properly.
2. In the mid-canto intros, he praises heroes whose actions teach us how to relate properly to others.
3. In the final-canto intros, as he prepares for the concluding celebration of the perfect marriage between Ruggiero and Bradamante, Ariosto gives unreserved praise to his colleagues (fellow poets and poetesses), and friends and tells us: "It's a wonderful life. The way we relate to one another is just fine, after all!"

I have no energy to discuss this system of moralizing thoroughly and the ways in which the official praise of Ariosto's bosses is woven into it. But let me give you a few examples from the beginning, middle and end of Ariosto's moralizing machine to show you what I'm talking about:

> Beginning: Three of the very early intros paint an extremely dim picture of relationships in the real world. All of them feature Ariosto's wonderful sense of humor but since I quoted both my authors more than enough last chapter, here I can—alas—only give you the message:
>
> Canto 2: Love is never ever requited in just the right way.

"Can Calvino's Humility Really Not Be Proud?"—127

> Canto 4: We have few if any real friends in a brutally hostile world
>
> Canto 5: Marriage, (the ideal love/friendship relationship in our culture) turns out to be a ferociously disappointing relationship in which psychological and physical warfare are inescapable.

So now we see that if the title and central episode of Ariosto's poem involves Orlando going mad, there's a good reason for this. I mean—it's natural for everyone to go mad if the world is as bad as Ariosto's Three Basic Reflections on Relationships suggest.

But in the middle cantos—just before Orlando actually goes mad—Ariosto begins to provide a solution. He gives us many lessons about how we can do our part to make the world a better place through unilateral acts of sacrifice that work against the conformist grain of rampant individual selfishness and vileness:

> Canto 19: Ariosto lauds Medoro's selfless devotion to his king
>
> Canto 20: Ariosto celebrates modern-day women and their achievements and shows how he himself, a man, can get over his fear of women
>
> Canto 21: Ariosto celebrates Zerbino for keeping his word

In the celebrations of Medoro and Zerbino, Ariosto contrasts these heroes with the typical people you meet in the Renaissance court environment—all mediocre success-oriented career people—and urges his readers to themselves become thoroughly unselfish good guys. In Canto 20 it is Ariosto himself, the writer-teacher who is the good example: in his praise of Marfisa, he demonstrates how remarkably easy it is for men to start treating woman as human beings and not scary sex objects.

Finally, towards the end of the *Orlando Furioso*, in three extended passages in the final part of the poem, Ariosto has nothing but good things to say about anyone he can think of:

> Canto 37 (1–20): Celebration of Vittoria Colonna (also Michelangelo's spiritual friend) but also celebrates many other women poets and the male poets that praise them
>
> Canto 42 (76–96): Celebration of favorite-circle-of-friend poets and their ladies
>
> Canto 46 (1–20): Celebration of all important male and female friends, especially intellectual ones, in the Northern Italian Aristocratic Universe (the only one that counts)

And one more thing: pretty much right in the middle of these passages is one of my favorite Ariosto intros, the one that opens canto 44 and celebrates true friendship as if to call special attention to the emphasis on the poet's own celebration of his friendships in the final cantos. Here the author and reader identify with two true friends from a humble urban ghetto environment (like Pin and Cousin in Calvino's first book). I simply can't resist quoting the beginning of this no matter how much my plan for this chapter doesn't really allow for it. Because the bad things Ariosto says about Renaissance courts are incredibly applicable to late 20th-century humanities departments where envious back-stabbers simply go berserk with joy when, for ANY reason at all they can justify voting "no" in a colleague's tenure or promotion case:

> Spesso in poveri alberghi e in picciol tetti,
> ne le calamitadi e nei disagi,
> meglio s'aggiungon d'amicizia i petti,
> che fra ricchezze invidiose et agi
> de le piene d'insidie e di sospetti
> corti regali e splendidi palagi,
> ove la caritade è in tutto estinta,
> né si vede amicizia, se non finta.
>
> (Often in poor dwellings and under crumbling roofs
> amid misfortunes and amid discomforts
> two breasts are joined in friendship closer
> than among the envying riches and the comforts
> of our palaces so full of treacheries
> of our courts of kings, so full of deceit
> where compassion is utterly vanished and gone
> and no friendship to be found that is not put on.)

"Can Calvino's Humility Really Not Be Proud?"—129

True friendship, then, is possible, even if rare outside of "poveri alberghi" and "picciol tetti" and somehow this must be the kind of friendship Ariosto and his friends have been able to establish against all odds that work against overly privileged people with cushy jobs and summers off to think too much.

I hope—those of you who didn't skip that last part of chap 4 I told you to skip—aren't a little bored. I mean in seeing that here I'm going to be doing the same thing as there: setting up Ariosto as phony positive and Calvino as phony negative and saying that they both amount to the same thing.

But let's go on: right now we have to fit Calvino's last book into the scheme I was just talking about in Ariosto

In *Palomar*—quickly in chapter 2—just like in canto two in Ariosto—we start considering the problem of how difficult relationships are. Calvino here narrates the failure of Mr. Palomar to relate to a topless nude female bather. Nothing serious was really at stake for Mr. P, but even a simple problem like how to walk past and casually look at a topless female bather proves infinitely complicated and ends in the worst possible misunderstanding between Mr. P and the female anatomy, I mean between Mr. P and the human being lying on the beach who happened to be a woman.

In the middle chapters we have some descriptions of relationships that might lead us to reflect on whether or not it is possible to learn how to relate properly to other people. In Calvino, you guessed it, all the models are negative and no solutions seem possible.

As in Ariosto, commenting on marriage has to be an important part of any meditation on relationships. And in the conversation between husband and wife in "il fischio del merlo" Calvino shows us what a typical exchange between wife and husband reveals about power struggles in marriage relationships. This "whistle of the blackbird" chapter is the most comical one in all of grim *Palomar* but the comedy doesn't really save us (or does it?) from some very depressing implications.

The (non)conversation between Mr. and Mrs. Palomar is a strange struggle-for-the-struggle's-sake in which each marriage "partner" battles to (re)assert superiority of some sort at every turn: an obviously senseless ritual way of conversing in which frightful underlying hostility and mutual incomprehension are the dominant aspect.

(And does Calvino say anything about conversations with kids? Not really: there is a daughter. But she seems to be just someone to give Mr. P an excuse to go to the zoo and identify with the lonely caged animals).

And what about friends? Especially intellectual associates of the sort Ariosto suggests he loves to hang out with? Well, we do have the friend he watches birds with . . . and that seems promising enough but boom! on p. 115, Mr. Palomar the intellectual quite suddenly refers with a desperate mutter of anguish to some "intellectual misadventures" that "aren't at all worth mentioning."The truth seems to be that he is extremely uncomfortable any time he is forced to interact with other intellectuals.

(Which, if you're interested, is always exactly how I feel after Scholarly Conventions in thinking over conversations or reactions (and mostly non-reactions) to the papers I read. But I understand how amid the endless stream of mumbled words accross the universe, minds succumb to drowsy wandering spells and all gets so lost. I have no idea why I still go to these things.)

So there's no consolation in real life, I mean in the unreal life of Palomar's world—Madness leads to that disconsolate brooding that of course is lurking behind Ariosto's too-easy happy go-lucky euphoric acceptance or everything and everybody at his poem's end. In fact the two approaches go together and one implies a movement towards the other: it can't be as good as in Ariosto but it can't be as bad in Calvino, either, can it?—

Wait a minute. I'm rushing things.

We haven't yet looked at Calvino's triple meditation at the End on how frustrating and impossible relationships with other human beings all are. His overturning with rhetorical disphoria Ariosto's rhetorical euphoria.

The last third of *Palomar*, "Mr. Palomar's silences" is all about all kinds of relationships not working out.

The basic problem is that one can't apply any sort of science of relationships to real life: Note the impossible conditional that introduces these remarks: "one would have to know":

> Di fronte a ogni persona uno dovrebbe sapere come situarsi in rapporto a essa, esser sicuro della reazione che ispira in lui la presenza dell'altro—avversione o attrazione, ascendente subito o imposto, curiosità o diffidenza o indifferen-

"Can Calvino's Humility Really Not Be Proud?"—131

za, dominio o sudditanza, discepolanza o magistero,—e in base a queste e alle controreazioni dell'altro stabilire le regole del gioco da applicare nella loro partita, le mosse e le contromosse da giocare.

(In order to figure out how to relate properly to others, one would have to know how to situate oneself in relation to that person, be sure of the reaction aroused in him (fem sic) by the presence of the other—aversion or attraction, influence accepted or imposed, curiosity or diffidence or indifference, domination or submission, disciplery or mastery—and based on these and on the counter-reactions of the other person establish the rules of play to apply in their game, the moves and the counter moves to play.)

Specifically, one can't at all help the young to avoid one's own mistakes:

Giovani/vecchi: "E' impossible tramettere l'esperienza, far evitare agli altri gli errori già commessi da noi"

(It is impossible to transmit experience, to help others avoid errors we ourselves once committed.)

In final analysis, one can't help anyone else or oneself to avoid mistakes or even to become slightly less impatient:

a tratti s'illude d'essersi liberato almeno dall'impazienza che l'ha accompagnato tutta la vita al vedere gli altri sbagliare in tutte le cose che fanno e al pensare che anche lui al loro posto sbaglierebbe non meno di loro ma comunque se ne renderebbe conto

(once in a while he deludes himself into thinking that he's at least become free of the impatience he's felt all his life when he's seen others make mistakes in everything they do and when he thinks that he too in their place would make mistakes no less than they but at least would realize it)

Absolute humility leads Palomar as near as possible to mad withdrawal from the world of the sane, in his mind if not necessarily in his actions. Madness is not only of the wild-raging tree-slinging sort we see in Orlando at the middle of *Orlando Furioso*. There is also the catatonic, paralysis in which one is either outright silent or speaks just to admit the great superiority of silence to non-silence.

So all that is left when one puts aside the official celebrations of co-workers, friends, bosses, and the people we are nearest to is an isolated brooding impatience with ourselves and everyone else. We are all mere "macchie d'inquietudine" ("brooding stains of unrest") with no hope of our unquiet St. Augustine hearts ever finding any rest.

But now we have to think for a minute about what this has to do with professors and their souls.

'Cause you know: the more one looks at late Calvino and especially *Palomar* and *If on a Winter's Night*, the more one is struck by how many professors there are everywhere, how much professors and their ridiculousnesses are a central subject in late Calvino. Think of *Winter*: first there's ridiculously named Professor Uzzi-Tuzzi and his rival Professor Galligani, the warring men in Chap 3 and 4, then there's the visiting lech prof in the telephone story and the Japanese senior full prof type in a kind of porno story that has all kinds of references to the stupid gossipy academic environment we professors work in. And then of course there's the professor-type readers at book's end. And even the Police captain in chapter 10 and of course, come to think of it, Silas and Hermes are really professors and of course Lotaria is the negative model of a typical late 20th-century prof that I wish he hadn't made a tedious feminist. (Do I really?)

And mostly Palomar (however much he tries to make fun of "stern preachy-teachy parents") is a stern preachy-teachy professor-father type obsessed with trying to teach student-children things that can really enrich their lives: maybe how to use models to think interesting things about inner and outer realities and or how to use models to at least think about improving society, if that's clearly as far as we intellectuals can go.

Calvino in his late books, is the writer-become-professor in order to best admit his failures. We all know professors are failures by definition. What people like me do is something anyone who has enough patience can do.

"Can Calvino's Humility Really Not Be Proud?"—133

Revelling in our classrooms in power we don't deserve, we professors create nothing and merely comment idly and uselessly on the same things professors before us through the centuries have commented on idly and uselessly.

Calvino the great writer presents himself as a failure of a professor whose only possible teaching can be the demonstration that it's impossible to even begin to figure out just what to teach and how.

What's at stake in writing *serious* fiction then, is always teaching: the reader is a student one wants to somehow lead in the right direction. Teaching another human being something important in a concrete teaching act, influencing another in some kind of right way would really be something significant. But Calvino comes to understand that writers and teachers have no real influence on anything:

> Il caso del signor Palomar è in realtà più semplice, in quanto la sua capacità d'influire su qualcosa o qualcuno è sempre stata trascurabile; il mondo può benissimo fare a meno di lui, e lui può considerarsi morto in tutta tranquillità senza nemmeno cambiare le sue abitudini.

> (Palomar's case is in reality simpler, insofar as his ability to influence something or somebody has always been negligible; the world can very well do without him and he can consider himself dead without even changing his habits.)

If Palomar is all writers and teachers who look at themselves in an undressed state without the usual (even if only partial) delusions of grandeur and importance —then what is my reaction to it?
Well I don't know, what's yours?
Personally, all I can say is this: in calling attentions to my own limitations in writing or speaking about myself, I am trying to move my reader/listeners to accept certain assumptions I need to make about myself and to give me certain set responses.
What assumptions and what set responses?
Well, the most important assumption I need you to accept is that I am somehow outside of the problem of power organization in society and that I somehow have the right to look at myself as more the victim than the victimizer in my failed relationships.

I need to have you acknowledge that I am a little better than the rest, more human, less a part of the problem than others around me. Even though I realize that you have nothing at all to learn from me, I want you to tell me it isn't so, that you've learned to think thoughtfully or even cheerfully about certain interesting and important problems and that that's enough as far as you're concerned.

Oh Yeah?

WHAT IF IT ISN'T?

You see, playing humility games is the best way for me to get you to tell me that somehow I'm not personally part of the problem. And you're getting something in return, aren't you? You're accepting my mediocrity and over-readiness to accept things as they are, and I'm helping you to accept your own mediocrity and confirming for you your own cherished view of yourself as someone who's also less a part of the problem than multitudes of other people.

Ariosto begins his story by telling Ippolito that he has very very little to give anybody and Calvino responds by ending Palomar characterizing himself as "a man as ill-equipped for understanding life as you can imagine" ("l'uomo più sprovveduto").

They both or course want us to contradict them. So do all teachers and writers who do insecurity routines. And everybody else for that matter.

Oh—you've already figured that out?

Importance importance importance. We all need to be important, don't we?

I just can't stop worrying about how important I am for others as a teacher and person. And how do the two categories relate in stupid ways in my life and in those of others, anyway? Isn't everyone always uselessly teaching her or his philosophy and major truths to others and finding them astonishingly uninterested?

(That's what this chapter should have been about if I could begin to approach the question of how teaching and its disappointments are relevant to people who don't teach for a living . . .)

Why worry about whether I've been important to anyone? Who me? A professor of a subject like Italian at a place like Loyola University of Chicago where Success-in-Career-and-Income Minded students (almost all of them) can't have any possible interest in foreign language and lit study?

(And haven't I shown my own interest in my own kind of career success by writing this book? Don't you hate academics who scoff at those in the non-academic professions?)

Isn't it all perfect? I know I AM unimportant and am universally treated as unimportant. What more could I want?

No no no, this isn't the point—what I need to do is make a list of people who've been important to me. I shouldn't worry about being important to others, but about telling all those who have been important to me (even if only slightly) that I'm appreciative of them.

But no! No one would believe what I said. They'd think I was praising them just so they'd praise me in return, not at all because I meant it.

So let me move quickly away from such deliberations: —I'm never going to worry about fishing for compliments or acknowledgements from other people. Never again. The whole business is too depressing.

I guess that's all I can come up with for now. And you're disappointed? Be thankful that disappointments from books are no big deal.

But there is one last question I have to take up, a question (I can pretend) Ariosto and Calvino are begging me in particular maybe to answer in a gratifying way for them is whether their books were somehow important for me, personally.

(I mean in spite of everything, in *Palomar*, Calvino is still somehow talking at the very end about important books and saying that after reading certain books you can at least change the way you look at your life, if nothing else. Even though he refuses to give any real examples or to talk about his own books.)

(Except there *is* one very curious reference on nearly the very last page. Calvino refers to the figure of a "just rebel" and this reference might suggest how Calvino understands his own lack of importance. Calvino knows he should have become some kind of "just rebel" instead of becoming a thoroughly establishment (as we used to say) professor-writer who deluded himself into believing irony and self-laceration games were enough.)

Hmmm? Well I have spent a lot of time with my two authors. No question about that. An entire decade. From the time I was 26 until the time I was 36, I've been reading or writing about one or the other or both of them.

(Dammit! It now suddenly occurs to me that I read them both too early. They're both authors to read between ages 35 and 45? or between 45 and 55? Or later, maybe . . . maybe even after death.)

But how should I answer the question about whether they're important to me or not?

You know—first thing I have to admit—you get tired of authors and their tricks, their obsessions, their limitations, you really do.

But are they really important to me? I mean besides giving me something to do on my job for awhile. (Isn't that enough, after all, something to keep you busy?)

Well, if you're not cheating and reading this last part before you should as I suspect you might be—you know I only found in Ariosto and Calvino what a below-average American born in the early 1950s could be expected to find.

So they weren't really important in changing me just as I haven't changed your way of thinking about them or anything else at all.

AND WHAT IF I DIDN'T REALLY WANT TO CHANGE YOU OR IMPROVE YOU OR YOUR LIFE AT ALL?

Well, if you're disappointed in me because there was nothing new and no clear message, know what I say? I say: I don't really like people who expect authors or teachers to tell them what to do with their lives or who expect someone to tell them whether to be optimistic or pessimistic—whether to hang in there and give it 110% or to whether to cultivate failure and not living up to one's potential. Everyone decides that one for herself and yes, everything's o.k. even not worrying about getting AIDS or committing suicide—if you really want my opinion.

I guess I'm supposed to end with a surprise and say something simple and life-affirming and literature-affirming and teaching-affirming. I mean, like "you, reader, of course realize that I wrote this book in the modest hope of making even only one person pick up Calvino—and God who knows? even forgotten-except-by-snobs Ariosto—and read and think about them—even just to make absolutely sure I'm totally full of shit in everything I say about them and the way I translate them."

But no, basically what I'm really getting at (or would possibly like to be getting at if there were any way of controlling such things) in this book is that people should feel less guilty about watching too much tv or about worrying so much about what other people think about their lack of maturity and sophistication or anything else for that matter. If only it were possible.

Because if I say: "I mean—does it really matter?"

And you answer: NO OF COURSE NOT

The conversation would have to go on as follows:

Me: You know, you're one of the 10 smartest people in the world. If I had the nerve I'd ask you to have sex with me.

You: I know. But I'm glad that in real life we can't help being so serious about ourselves and things like sex and stuff because it's somehow funnier that way, don't you think?

May 1987-July 1988

INDEX OF NAMES AND SUBJECTS

All My Children: 18
Angelica: 14, 33, 34, 35, 39–40, 47, 53, 54, 61, 67, 68, 73, 74, 78, 79, 103, 104
Arab terrorists: 63
Astolpho: 14, 80–85, 108

Barnes, Julian: 114
Beach Boys: 27–29, 69
Boiardo, Matteo Maria: 20–23, 25
Bradamante: 14, 33–35, 36, 39, 40, 41, 44, 47, 48, 49, 51, 53, 54, 56, 58, 62–64, 68, 73, 114, 116, 118–22
Brand Name Scholarly Book Publishers: 55
Brand Name Institutions: 89
Bush, George: 63

confessions, phoniness of: 115
Comp Lit snobs: 72, 79
conventionality: 11–13, 114
Cervantes: 20–22, 25–26, 71–72, 105
Colonna, Vittoria: 128

Dante: 90
d'Este, Cardinal Ippolito: 39, 101–02, 117, 134
Disney, Walt: 39
Duke, The: 71
Dylan, Bob: 90, 118

feminism, bashing of: 32, 36
feminism, history of: 29
feminism, praise of: 45–46

feminism, unimportance of: 29
fellowship competitions, solution to problem of: 107
fellowship competitions, unfairness of: 107–08
Ferraro, Geraldine: 63
French philosophy, limitations of: 9, 32, 73, 76

German philosophy, limitations of: 32, 73
Goethe: 91

Joyce, James: 11

Italian culture, superior sophistication of: 32

Lennon, John: 13
Levi, Primo: 26
Loyola University of Chicago 1963 NCAA Championship Basketball Team: 115

Madonna: 19
male bashing: 113
male feminists, phoniness of: 31
Manganelli, Giorgio: 26
Marxists, banality of: 12
Medoro: 19–20, 34, 73, 74, 79, 127
men, bashing of: 15, 43, 69, 71, 83, 109, 114

men, history of: 61
men, praise of: 43
men, unimportance of: 132–33
Milton, Giovanni: 71

nudity: 54, 60, 63, 64, 114

Oprah: 39
Orlando: 14, 60, 61, 70, 72–80, 82, 84, 85, 116, 132
O Shaughnessy, Brigid: 32, 90

Pantheon: 115
paranoia: 36, 61, 73, 107, 128
Pasolini, Pier Paolo: 12
pessoptimism: 112–13, 129, 136
philistinism, anti-intellectual: 73, 76
Piscopo, Joe: 81
Prince: 109
professoriality: 11–13, 24
professors, castles of illusions of: 36, 62, 125

publish or persish: 11–13

Raphael: 19–20
Rodomonte: 42, 43, 122–25
Rossellini: 68

Shandling, Gary: 5, 92
Shields, Brooke: 65
silence: 70
Simon, Paul: 61, 104
Soldier Field: 20
Song of Roland: 18
Springsteen, Bruce: 45, 90
Stallone, Slyvester: 71
study abroad programs, pointlessness of : 21–22, 65

Talking Heads: 74

Wayne, John: see: Duke, The
word processors: 6, 68, 69, 97
women, insulting of all: 56, 124

Zimmerman, Robert : 90, 118